Ancient Egypt in 101 Questions and Answers

Ancient Egypt in 101 Questions and Answers

Thomas Schneider

Translated by David Lorton

Edited by JJ Shirley

Cornell University Press
Ithaca, NY

The original German edition of this book, *Die 101 wichtigsten Fragen. Das Alte Ägypten*, was published by Verlag C.H. Beck in Germany. Copyright © Verlag C.H. Beck oHG, München 2010

English translation copyright © 2013 by Thomas Schneider

English translation first published 2013 by I.B.Tauris & Co Ltd in the United Kingdom

English translation first published in the United States of America 2013 by Cornell University Press

First published 2013 by Cornell University Press

Printed and bound in Great Britain by T.J. International, Padstow, Cornwall

Library of Congress Cataloging-in-Publication Data

Schneider, Thomas, 1964– author.
  [Alte Ägypten. English]
  Ancient Egypt in 101 questions and answers / Thomas Schneider ; translated by David Lorton ; edited by J.J. Shirley.
     pages cm
  Includes bibliographical references and index.
  ISBN 978-0-8014-5254-3 (cloth : alk. paper)
  1. Egypt--Civilization--To 332 B.C.--Miscellanea. 2. Egypt--Social life and customs--To 332 B.C.--Miscellanea. I. Lorton, David, 1945- translator. II. Shirley, J. J., editor. III. Schneider, Thomas, 1964- Alte Ägypten. Translation of: IV. Title. V. Title: Ancient Egypt in one hundred one questions and answers.

  DT61.S32513 2013
  932'.01--dc23

                           2013010646

Cloth printing   10 9 8 7 6 5 4 3 2 1

Contents

Illustrations

Timeline

PREHISTORY	PREDYNASTIC	EARLY DYNASTIC		
700,000–4000 BCE	4000–2950 BCE	2950–2670 BCE	2670–2600 BCE	2600–2 BCE
Palaeolithic and Neolithic	Regional cultures	Dynasties 1 and 2	Dynasty 3	Dynast

MIDDLE KINGDOM			SECOND INTERMEDIATE PERIOD	
2040–1990 BCE	1990–1809 BCE	1809–1640 BCE	1640–1532 BCE	1548–13(BCE
Dynasty 11	Dynasty 12	Dynasties 13 and 14	Dynasties 15, 16 and 17	Dynasty

D KINGDOM			FIRST INTERMEDIATE PERIOD	
80–2350 BCE	2350–2200 BCE	2200–2168 BCE	2168–2030 BCE	2130–1990 BCE
ynasty 5	Dynasty 6	Dynasty 8	Dynasties 9 and 10	Dynasty 11

KINGDOM		THIRD INTERMEDIATE PERIOD	LATE PERIOD	GRAECO-ROMAN PERIOD
2–1198 BCE	1198–1086 BCE	1086–664 BCE	664–332 BCE	332 BCE– 395 CE
asty 19	Dynasty 20	Dynasties 21, 22, 23, 24 and 25	Dynasties 26, 27, 28, 29 and Second Persian Period	Macedonian, Ptolemaic and Roman rulers

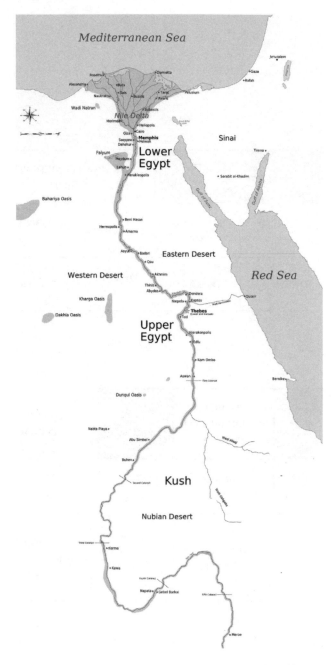

Map of Ancient Egypt (by Jeff Dahl)

Preface

Ancient Egypt so captures people's imagination that innumerable questions can be asked about its civilization, and in many cases we can discern the answers, while in others they are yet to be discovered. The Classical world of Greece and Rome perceived ancient Egypt as a fount of wisdom. From then until the European Renaissance there was a belief that those initiated in ancient Egypt's secrets would find there the answers to the world's mysteries, and Renaissance thinkers even viewed the Egyptian language as the perfect, divine speech of the first men. No other ancient culture has fascinated so many, even in our own day. Exhibitions of Egyptian art and archaeological discoveries in the "land of the Nile" continue to generate interest and amazement, while Egyptian motifs appear in architecture, literature, in art works, and in films. For adherents of the esoteric, Egypt is a central reference point. Since its inception in the nineteenth century, Egyptology has established itself as an academic discipline on all continents, focused on the study and interpretation of ancient Egypt's texts and material remains, as well as the preservation and presentation of this heritage to the world.

Today, scholars and the general public view ancient Egypt as one of the most important—and fascinating—ancient civilizations of humankind. Egyptologists do not ask the same questions as tourists. Many of the questions gathered in this book are included because of the frequency with which they are asked, while others can provide surprising, unusual, and perhaps even provocative insights into ancient Egypt. Taken together, they aim to introduce readers to ancient Egypt and invite them to further study this millennia-old, and still intriguing, culture. The book's cover illustrates the broader themes into which the questions posed here have been grouped. It depicts the harpist of Amun, Djed-khonsu-iuf-ankh, playing in front of the god of the universe, Re-Harakhti. The image comes from a stela in the Louvre, one of the large Egyptian collections established in the time of modern colonial rule in Egypt (Part 1). Re-Harakhti's seat has the shape of an Egyptian hieroglyph with which *Maat*, the most essential concept of the Egyptian world view, could be written (Part 2). The stela dates to the Third Intermediate Period, a time of political fragmentation (Part 3), and is a document of personal religion (Part 4), a work of art (Part 5), inscribed in hieroglyphs written in two directions (Part 6), and features a temple musician from the lower segment of Egyptian society (Part 7).

This book is dedicated to the memory of David Lorton, Egyptologist and translator, without whose effort this book—the last one he translated—would not have appeared. Egyptology and all enthusiasts of ancient Egypt will always remember him for his dedication to making important books of German and French Egyptologists accessible to an English-speaking public, thereby reaching thousands of readers across the globe. David's English text was somewhat adjusted and some articles substituted before JJ Shirley generously edited the manuscript for the press. I am also thankful to Alex Higson from I.B.Tauris for supervising the production process of the manuscript, and especially to Jonathan McDonnell, Managing Director of I.B.Tauris, for the opportunity of publishing the book with the publishing house, and for his thoughtful comments on the manuscript.

1

Ancient Egypt and the Modern World

1.

Does our life follow an ancient Egyptian cycle?

Today we take our calendar year, with its 4 seasons, 12 months, 52 weeks, and 365 days, for granted. This calendar has its roots in the solar calendar of ancient Egypt. The length of our year results from the apparent movement of the sun around the earth. It lasts about 365.24219 days, though it was a bit longer in ancient Egyptian times, for the rotation of the earth is gradually slowing down. Using a calendar based on the solar year allows for a precise correlation with the seasons. A shorter lunar calendar of 354 days was favored by most other civilizations of the ancient Near East. In ancient Egypt, the reference point for the beginning of the Egyptian year was the rising of Sothis (the star Sirius) after seventy-five days of invisibility, which corresponded roughly with the beginning of the Nile inundation in mid-July. Sothis was thus understood as the bringer of the inundation, which was of critical importance for agriculture and for Egypt's very existence. There has been considerable debate as to whether the rising of Sirius was used for this purpose when the calendar was first devised. Because the Egyptian year of exactly 365 days continually shifted with respect to the slightly longer so-called tropical year of about 365.24219 days, this would only allow for a date when the heliacal (*i.e.*, just before the sun) rising of Sothis corresponded to the beginning of the solar year. This was in the third millennium, between 2772 and 2769 BCE, though earlier Egyptologists viewed the previous correspondence in 4240 BCE as the "oldest date in human history," as Eduard Meyer put it. Today, a later date for the introduction of the calendar, between the time of the Naqada II culture (c.3300 BCE) and the beginning of Dynasty 3 (c.2700 BCE), seems more plausible. Equally of ancient Egyptian origin is our division of the year into twelve months. However, the Egyptians divided their year into three seasons of four months, each with thirty days, based on the Egyptian seasonal cycle. This grouping amounted to only 360 days, leaving five additional days at the end of the year, the so-called epagomenal days. These days were understood as the birthdays of the gods of the Osiris myth, and they were also thought to be a critical transitional phase that had to be controlled by means of rituals. These rituals were referred to in ancient Egyptian as "rituals of the New Year" because they marked the beginning of the next year, just as our own New Year's celebrations do (see also Question 91). The three Egyptian seasons, which corresponded to the phases of the agricultural year, were called Inundation, Sowing, and Summer (Harvest). But these designations according to the agricultural cycle quickly became irrelevant, for the Egyptian (civil) year was nearly a quarter of a day shorter than the actual year, with the result that there was a growing discrepancy between the two, amounting to about one day every four years and one month every 120 years. The introduction of an additional "leap day" under Ptolemy III (in his Canopus Decree, 238 BCE) did not catch on. It was not until Julius Caesar's calendrical reform in 46 BCE that an improved form of the Egyptian solar calendar replaced the older calendar used in Rome and the necessary correction made its way to Egypt. This "Julian calendar" was in its turn replaced by the "Gregorian calendar" promulgated by Pope Gregory XIII in 1582, though the former is used to this day by the Orthodox Church. Interestingly, the calendar of the French Revolution, which was in use from 1793 to 1805, also consisted of twelve months of thirty days, with five (in leap years, six) additional days, and even a monthly division of three ten-day "decades," following an Egyptian model. The original Egyptian calendar, with its Egyptian-Coptic month names, is still employed today by the Coptic Church, the Christian church of Egypt (see also Question 68).

Unlike the modern division of the year into weeks of seven days, each Egyptian month was divided into three "decades" of ten days each, the last one or two of which were days off from work, thus constituting a "weekend." These decades were named after the gods Re, Osiris, and Horus and were defined as the span of time during which a specific lodestar (a decan) was visible in the first hour of the night. The modern concept of a "24-hour day" can be traced to both ancient Babylonia and Egypt, where day and night were each divided into twelve hours. In New Kingdom Egypt (1535–1070 BCE) this structure of time received symbolic representation in the Books of the Netherworld. These books divide the afterlife (the realm of the dead) into twelve sections, each of which the sun god sails through in the course of an hour. The Book of Gates depicts the twelve goddesses of the night hours. Here, a snake symbolizing time has the name "Passing One, who gives birth to twelve snakes that are annihilated again by her after they have swallowed the hours." Another scene depicts a god called "Braider," who produces a rope with twelve coils representing the hours and then swallows it again coil after coil. The day also had its twelve hour goddesses, and as the sun god traversed the day his form changed hourly, marking his passage across the sky.

2.

Why did Lord Byron and Percy Bysshe Shelley write about Cheops and Ramesses?

The rediscovery of Egypt by the Napoleonic expedition (1798–1801) marks not only the birth of Egyptology as an academic discipline, it also sparked a huge general interest in the past of Egypt and its antiquities. Napoleon's army was accompanied by 150 scholars who were commissioned to comprehensively survey the geography, nature, antiquities and customs of the country. The monumental publication of their research, the *Description de l'Egypte* (published in several volumes beginning in 1810) represents the first modern survey of an entire country and its past ruins. One result of this campaign was that Egypt's monuments and artifacts were rapidly becoming known to the European public, and Romantic poets of the early nineteenth century commonly referred to the grandeur and demise of Egypt's past. After the French were defeated in 1801, the British confiscated the antiquities collected in Egypt by the French expedition and transferred them to the British Museum. Among them was the Rosetta stone, which is still regarded as among the most famous artifacts of the museum's Egyptian collection, and an icon of ancient Egyptian culture; the Rosetta stone also played an important part in the decipherment of hieroglyphs. In the years that followed, Henry Salt, the British Consul General of Egypt during the rule of Viceroy Mohamed Ali Pasha, was the main acquirer of antiquities for the British Museum. In 1817, with the help of

Giovanni Battista Belzoni, a former circus strongman and later discoverer of Egyptian monuments, Salt had the upper part of a colossal statue of Ramesses II removed from Ramesses' funerary temple in Western Thebes and erected at the British Museum. The artifacts on display at the British Museum spurred unprecedented public and scholarly enthusiasm and poetic imagination of the antiquity of Egypt.

The leading Romantic poets who likely saw the upper part of Ramesses' colossal statue at the museum reflected on Egypt in their works. Perhaps the most famous of these is Percy Bysshe Shelley (1792–1822) whose sonnet "Ozymandias" (the Greek form of the throne name of Ramesses II, Usermaatre) from 1817 was inspired by the actual statue, depictions of the broken statue of Ramesses II at the Ramesseum, and the Classical author Diodorus Siculus:

> I met a traveller from an antique land,
> Who said, 'Two vast and trunkless legs of stone
> Stand in the desert. Near them, on the sand,
> Half sunk, a shattered visage lies, whose frown,
> And wrinkled lip, and sneer of cold command,
> Tell that its sculptor well those passions read,
> Which yet survive, stamped on these lifeless things,
> The hand that mocked them and the heart that fed.
> And on the pedestal these words appear:
> "My name is Ozymandias, King of Kings.
> Look on my works ye Mighty, and despair!"
> No thing beside remains. Round the decay
> Of that Colossal Wreck, boundless and bare,
> The lone and level sands stretch far away.'

What Shelley emphasizes here is that the vanity of tyrannical power is defeated by time, providing a warning to modern tyrants. The truth about the arrogance of the King is revealed by the sculptor and has survived the mighty King's ultimate transience by thousands of years, just as the despair that the tyrant intended to instill in his rivals for power inevitably befell himself. More than referring just to the King, the statue of

Ozymandias also stands for the demise of the ancient civilization of Egypt, and for the ultimate end of *any* civilization. In the sonnet "On a Stupendous Leg of Granite" that Shelley's poet-friend Horace Smith (1779–1849) wrote at the same time as Shelley, the passage on Egypt's Ozymandias is followed by this stanza:

> We wonder, —and some Hunter may express
> Wonder like ours, when thro' the wilderness
> Where London stood, holding the Wolf in chace,
> He meets some fragment huge, and stops to guess
> What powerful but unrecorded race
> Once dwelt in that annihilated place.

In this vein, their common friend Lord Byron (1788–1824) wrote in the first *canto* of Don Juan in 1818:

> What are the hopes of man? Old Egypt's King
> Cheops erected the first pyramid
> And largest, thinking it was just the thing
> To keep his memory whole, and mummy hid;
> But somebody or other rummaging,
> Burglariously broke his coffin's lid:
> Let not a monument give you or me hopes,
> Since not a pinch of dust remains of Cheops.

3.

Why is there a pyramid on the American dollar bill?

The front of the American dollar bill bears a portrait of George Washington. The back displays both sides of the Great Seal of the United States, which was worked on by three different committees between 1776 and 1782. On the back of the seal, and of the bill, is a thirteen-stepped, incomplete pyramid, above which hovers a triangle bearing the eye of divine Providence. The number thirteen refers to the original number of the states of the Union, and it appears more than once on the front of the seal: the thirteen stars above the eagle, the thirteen stripes on the shield in front of it, and the thirteen arrows it holds in its talons. This was not the first use of the pyramid on American money—it also appeared in 1778 on the fifty dollar bill of the Continental currency. According to the explanation provided to Congress, the pyramid symbolizes the "strength and duration" of America.

The idea that the presence of the pyramid on the dollar bill is a reference to Freemasonry is unlikely. Egyptian symbolism entered into Freemasonry only during the eighteenth century, especially following the publication of Abbé Jean Terrasson's novel *Sethos* (1731), with its description of an initiation into the mysteries of Isis inside the Great Pyramid of Giza, and with the "Egyptian Masonry" established by Count Cagliostro in 1780. The artistic high point of this esoteric turn to Egypt was Mozart's opera *The Magic Flute*, which was first performed in 1791. Although Benjamin Franklin was a Freemason, he served only on the first committee that worked on the Great Seal.

The other members of the committee were the later presidents
John Adams and Thomas Jefferson, neither of whom were
Masons, and none of their sketches included a pyramid. To the
contrary, Franklin's original idea for the back of the Seal was
Pharaoh's death by drowning in the Red Sea and the freeing
of the Israelites from their bondage in Egypt, along with the
"pillar of fire" as a symbol of God's presence and the motto,
"rebellion against tyrants is obedience to God." The pyramid
thus seems to have been used, as it had been since antiquity, as
a symbol for permanence.

 # 4.

Why is ancient Egypt so central to Afrocentrism?

Egypt is mostly viewed as a Near Eastern culture, and even modern Egypt is primarily understood as part of the Middle East and the Mediterranean world. At the same time, however, Egypt is a part of the African continent and as such represents its oldest civilization. The Afrocentric political movement, which has been especially important in the United States and France, lays claim to Egypt as a black African culture. Its adherents call on traditional scholarship to acknowledge that this more African ancient Egypt was not only superior to classical Greek culture, but also that all western culture derives from Egypt, a fact they say is denied by Eurocentric scholarship. Yet it seems that this Afrocentric fixation on Europe and the west is actually itself Eurocentric and western, and not genuinely African. Far from being a phenomenon of the late twentieth century, the origins of Afrocentric historiography reach back into the early nineteenth century, arising out of the vehement debates over black people's capacity for culture and the abolition of slavery in the USA. At that time, one of the arguments made by black writers and political activists was that civilization originated in Ethiopia and Egypt, and only later was transmitted to Greece. More recently, Professor Martin Bernal of Cornell University sought to substantiate the Afrocentric thesis in his famous book *Black Athena*, again bringing the debate over ancient Egypt's connection with black Africa into focus. Though Bernal correctly demonstrates that classical history has been reconstructed with a Eurocentric bias, his attempt to derive classical civilization from Egypt and Phoenicia must be judged a failure. Outside the Sudan (ancient Nubia), there is no evidence that black Africa was much influenced by ancient Egypt, an influence alleged by such important Afrocentrists as Sheikh Anta Diop and his disciples. Nevertheless, many questions posed to Egyptology by Afrocentrism are important, especially concerning what modern European concepts Egyptology has projected onto ancient Egypt, for Egyptology has certainly always been a white, primarily European and North American, discipline. Today, there is a growing openness to dialogue. To give one example, the noted Egyptologist Jan Assmann has recently written the preface to an Afrocentric book that seeks the origin of "*Maat*," the Egyptian concept of order, in black Africa (see **Question 39**).

Figure 1: Ancient Egypt as an inspiration for modern architecture: The 'Egyptian Building' in Richmond, Virginia. Built in 1845 for the Medical College of Virginia, now part of the Medical Center of Virginia Commonwealth University

# 5.

Why does Egypt appear
in the Jewish doctrine?

Egypt is the only ancient high culture mentioned in the doctrine of a monotheistic world religion: in the *Shema Yisrael* (hear, O Israel!), Israel is admonished not to forget that God freed Israel from bondage in Egypt (Deuteronomy 6:12). The departure for the Promised Land is a central element in the salvation history of Israel, and the historical confirmation that Israel was God's Chosen People. In old formulaic phrases, this god is linked to the exodus from Egypt: "I am the Lord your God from the land of Egypt" (Hosea 12:9; 13:4). By way of the Old Testament, this image of Egypt found its way into Christian and Muslim conceptions of the world, especially the negative image of Pharaoh as a godless despot. This tradition reflects the strong connection between the histories of Israel and Egypt. As the civilization located directly to its southwest, Egypt was an enduring reference point for Israel, and Egyptian amulets and craft objects were widespread in Israel and Palestine during the first millennium BCE. Since Egypt was hardly ever able to exercise influence over Israel in the first millennium, the prophet Jeremiah has an Assyrian general, standing before Jerusalem, deride Egypt as a broken reed on which King Hezekiah can no longer rely (Jeremiah 36:6). Nevertheless, Egypt remained an object of fascination, and even a source of theological inspiration (see **Question 82**). The biblical story of Joseph and his brothers portrays Egypt as a land of cultural achievements and economic prosperity.

In the nineteenth century, the desire to know more about the historical circumstances of the Israelites' stay in Egypt was one of the incentives in the establishment of Egyptology as a discipline. Interest focused in particular on the archaeological investigation of the eastern Nile Delta, where scholars expected to find indications of the Israelites' sojourn in Egypt and their flight from that country. Today there is still much debate over whether the events of the patriarchal narratives and the Exodus story actually took place. Most scholars of the Hebrew Bible acknowledge that these narratives, emphasizing Israel's selection by Yahwe, are of relatively late origin. The question of Israel's beginnings was not relevant until it was an established state in the Near East during the first millennium—that is, many centuries after the supposed sojourn in Egypt. In fact, it was not until the very end of the second millennium that Israel coalesced out of various population groups extant in Palestine and assumed the name of "Israel" from one of these earlier groups. The first attestation of this name comes from the text of the so-called Israel Stela of the Egyptian King Merneptah (c.1200 BCE). The Exodus from Egypt thus cannot have occurred in the form depicted in the biblical retrospective. Even important details of the biblical narrative, such as Ramses and Pithom, the cities which were supposedly built by the Israelites in bondage, and the name Moses, do not hold water. And yet, the theme is so centrally anchored in the biblical tradition that it scarcely seems plausible that we should dismiss the Exodus as a pure invention of the period of the Babylonian Exile, when the deported Israelites were supposedly in need of a historical precedent for a renewed liberation. Most scholars therefore hold to the possibility that Moses and a small group of emigrants really existed. Migrations to and from Egypt, as well as the rise of foreigners to the highest offices of the Egyptian state, are well attested (see also **Questions 32** and **83**). A small group of people may have migrated from Egypt into Palestine where they merged with the local Israel group for whom the memory of the immigrants from Egypt became a particularly important component of their cultural identity.

 **6.**

What role does ancient Egypt play in the Mormon faith?

Ancient Egypt plays a prominent role in the tradition of the Church of Jesus Christ of the Latter-Day Saints, more commonly known as the Mormons. Joseph Smith, the founder and first prophet of the church, claimed that in 1823 he had a vision of an angel named Moroni, who revealed to him that a book written on golden plates was to be found in Hill Cumorah in the state of New York. These plates, which Smith said he recovered in 1827, were supposedly inscribed in "reformed Egyptian," which he himself translated with the help of two oracular stones called Urim and Thummim that he found along with the plates. The text of the plates constitutes the content of the Book of Mormon. There was no writing system called "reformed Egyptian," however, and the few preserved lines of a transcription of the golden plates (the so-called Anthon transcript) bear no resemblance to the signs of the Egyptian writing system (see **Questions 70** and **72**). It should also be noted that in 1827, no one in North America was familiar with Jean-François Champollion's successful decipherment of the hieroglyphs in 1822. In addition, at that early date, knowledge of the grammar of the Egyptian language was still too rudimentary to permit the translation of any ancient Egyptian texts.

Along with the Book of Mormon, which was published in 1830, the canonical scriptures of the church include the Book of Abraham, which Joseph Smith claimed to have translated from an Egyptian papyrus he acquired in 1835; this book was allegedly the biography of the biblical patriarch Abraham. The papyrus was long presumed to have been lost, but after it was rediscovered in 1967 in the collection of the Metropolitan Museum of Art, scholars determined that it was a manuscript of a Ptolemaic era funerary text, the so-called "Book of Breathing." This Egyptian text does not, however, have anything to do with the biblical patriarch. The figure identified by Joseph Smith as Abraham is actually a deceased person lying on a bier, or perhaps the funerary god Osiris himself. As for the illustrations on the papyrus, Joseph Smith altered some of them and added others in his rendering. Although the Mormons still believe in the veracity of these documents, outside the church, Smith's alleged translation of the two texts from ancient Egyptian is today seen as a phenomenon of the fascination with Egypt in early nineteenth-century America (see Figure 1).

Figure 2: A symbol of Egyptian religion's rivalry with, and influence on, Christianity: the uninscribed Vatican Obelisk, removed from Egypt in the reign of Augustus

7.

Why is there a Pope in Rome and not the High Priest of Isis?

At the center of the Catholic Church in St. Peter's Square in Rome stands a monument of ancient Egyptian religion: the (uninscribed) Vatican Obelisk, with a Christian cross added at its top (Figure 2). In the reign of the emperor Augustus, this obelisk was taken to Alexandria by Gaius Cornelius Gallus, the first Roman prefect of Egypt. In the first century CE the emperor Caligula had the obelisk brought to Rome and set up in his new Circus, which was located on the site of present-day St. Peter's Basilica. Connected by legend with the martyrdom of Saint Peter, the obelisk came to be called the "pyramid of blessed Peter." In 1586, Pope Sixtus V had it moved, at great cost, to its present location. The obelisk reminds us that in Roman times there was always the possibility that the Isis cult, and not Christianity, would become the official religion of Rome. As late as the sixteenth century, Giordano Bruno, who was condemned to death as a heretic by the Catholic Church in 1600, complained that the "good religion" of the Egyptians had been destroyed by Christianity.

During the Hellenistic Period, Isis became increasingly worshipped across the Mediterranean, and by the second century BCE had risen to the status of a universal deity throughout the Hellenistic world. In the period of the Roman Empire she was nascent Christianity's most powerful rival. Her cult in Graeco-Roman times was Egyptianizing, not Egyptian, and enriched by non-Egyptian elements, such as being revered as mistress of fate and goddess of victory. Isis cults, Isis mysteries, and even novels about Isis (the most famous today being Apuleius' *Golden Ass*) spread through the entire empire. Several emperors—Caligula, Claudius, Nero, Otho, Vespasian, Domitian—built important temples to Isis in Rome and elsewhere (*e.g.*, Beneventum), and promoted her cult. In the second century, Hadrian, who harbored an antipathy towards Christianity, visited Egypt and thereafter felt closely connected to Egyptian religion. Following the death of his lover Antinous, who drowned in the Nile, Hadrian founded the city of Antinoopolis near the site of Antinous' death, and instituted a cult of Osiris-Antinous. At Hadrian's villa in Tibur/Tivoli, he commissioned Egyptian structures and a cult of Osiris of Canopus, who embodied the waters of the Nile. Marcus Aurelius, whose army on the Danube was supposedly saved from destruction by an Egyptian magician in 172 (the so-called "Rain Miracle on the Danube"), and Septimius Severus also visited Egypt. Commodus personally served as an officiant of the Egyptian cult of Isis. Bearing the title Philosarapis ("loving Sarapis"), Caracalla promoted the cult of the Graeco-Egyptian god Sarapis throughout the Roman Empire, and in Rome he lifted the ban on Egyptian cults within the city walls. Diocletian, who saw himself as the custodian of ancient beliefs, decreed a major persecution of Christians in 303; to this day, the Coptic Church of Egypt regards 284, his first year of reign, as the beginning of its calendrical era (the Era of the Martyrs). Eventually, in the fourth century, Constantine, after defeating his rival Licinius, who still adhered to the Egyptian cult, attributed his victory to Christianity and became the first Christian emperor of Rome. At around the same time, though, the Neoplatonists Porphyry and Iamblichus were still praising Egypt as the land of genuine contact with the gods and their mysteries. For centuries, there was thus another option in the history of the world. If Isis worship had been elevated to the status of the official religion of the Roman Empire, there would now be a high priest of Isis sitting in Rome, and theologians would be studying not Christian, but ancient Egyptian texts.

 # 8.

What is the importance of ancient Egypt for modern Egypt?

In the 1920s and 1930s—in contrast to the preceding period and the more recent past—modern Egypt's Muslim elite began to view ancient Egypt and ancient Egyptians as an important part of their cultural history. This connection between modern and ancient played an integral role in the ousting of British rule, and in the course of Egypt's growing national consciousness the culture of the pharaohs was represented as a counterculture to the western world. Egypt's ancient glory was also interpreted as a way to stimulate the renewal of modern Egypt—an attitude that gained further inspiration from the discovery of the tomb of Tutankhamun in 1922. This phenomenon found outward expression in Egyptianizing architecture, such as the Giza railway station and the mausoleum built in 1928 for Saad Zaghlul Pasha. Pasha was the hero of the 1919 uprising against British rule and founder of the Wafd party, and claimed in his speeches to be inspired by the glory and the achievements of ancient Egypt. Ahmed Shawqi (1868–1932), Egypt's "prince among poets," accorded a prominent place to ancient Egypt in his stage plays. Ignoring the actual historical ruptures over the course of the millennia, much emphasis was placed on Egypt's historical and ethnic continuity from the Old Kingdom to the twentieth century, as well as the unity of Muslim and Christian Egyptians. A leading intellectual of this Egyptian-pharaonic nationalism was Husayn Fawzi. In *An Egyptian Sindbad*, a brilliant assessment of Egypt's historical identity published in 1961, he stressed the indelible character of Egypt, which reached its peak in pharaonic times, before influences from outside impeded the development of the genius of its people.

After the downfall of King Farouk in the Egyptian revolution of 1952, the ideology of Arab nationalism increasingly conflicted with this search for identity in ancient Egypt. The tension between the two points of view found symbolic expression after the presidency of Anwar el-Sadat, whose return to pharaonic Egypt as a source of inspiration for modern Egypt came to an end with his assassination in 1981. His assassin, Khalid Islambouli, testified during his trial that he had shot "Pharaoh." Playing on Muslim understanding, he identified Sadat with Pharaoh as the historical prototype of a tyrant. The Unknown Soldier Memorial with Sadat's tomb in Cairo recalls the shape of a pyramid, thus intimating the importance of ancient Egypt to modern Egypt.

Although the pharaonic past as a tourist attraction is one of contemporary Egypt's most important sources of income, it has yet to become an integral part of the Egyptian sense of identity, in the way Egyptian banknotes depict both ancient and Muslim monuments and thus suggest such a twofold identity. There are no local historical societies promoting public interest in ancient Egypt, a reflection of the cultural rupture caused by the Muslim conquest of Egypt in the year 641 CE, and also of European control and influence in the development of the modern management of its archaeological heritage (see also **Questions 20** and **66**). Ancient Egypt is taught in the schools and through field trips, but it is not part of children's upbringing in Muslim homes. At most, it is part of the identity of a small elite, represented, for example, by the novel *Akhenaten, Dweller in Truth* by Naguib Mahfouz, a winner of the Nobel Prize for literature. But there is also a dividing line in this respect between Muslim and Christian (Coptic) Egypt, for the Copts understand themselves to be heirs to ancient Egypt (see **Question 68**). Nonetheless, remnants of ancient Egyptian rituals persist even in contemporary Muslim Egypt—for instance, in burial customs and the veneration of saints.

# 9.

What role did Egyptology play in the Third Reich?

After seizing power in Germany in 1933, the Nazi regime took measures aimed at bringing universities into line and changing the professoriate and the subject matters taught according to the spirit of the new ideology. Jewish and politically disloyal instructors were expelled from the faculties and persecuted. The totalitarian constraints placed on scholarship affected many disciplines, and those whose research areas could not be made to conform were pronounced illegitimate. In 1935, a Nazi scholar at Leipzig University, the ancient historian Helmut Berve, disputed the right of Egyptology to exist in the German university system because it dealt with a civilization that was "non-Aryan" and "alien to the German racial ideal" to the point of incomprehensibility. Egyptologists protested this verdict, while at the same time some attempted to portray Egypt as a quasi-"Aryan" culture. These scholars claimed that the notion of "blood and soil" was crucial to Egyptian culture, that the racial community and not the individual was of overriding importance (see **Questions 83 and 84**). They stressed that Pharaoh, as Egypt's charismatic "Führer" and embodiment of the ideal of a master race, led Egypt and its people to their fateful destiny as an ancient world power. The imperialistic state of the New Kingdom was viewed as the climax of Egyptian culture, while the "pollution of Egyptian blood" through Semitic infiltration was claimed to be responsible for weakening Egypt's racial substance and for Egypt's alleged decline in the first millennium BCE (see also **Questions 24, 32 and 35**).

Many Egyptologists who could not continue their scholarly work in Germany emigrated to the USA or to Israel, where they introduced important new research directions, while others lost their positions in Germany or were prevented from receiving a doctorate. Although the Institutes of Egyptology in Munich and Bonn were particularly anti-Nazi in their orientation, many Egyptologists were active National Socialists (members of the Nazi party, the SA, and the SS) and supporters of Nazi policies—for example, Hermann Grapow, Professor of Egyptology at the University of Berlin. Outside of Germany, the German Archaeological Institute in Cairo played an important foreign policy role until it was closed in September 1939. Some of the Egyptologists who were dismissed from their universities in 1945 for being pro-Nazi were, however, able to resume professorial positions in the 1950s and 1960s.

10.

Can Egyptology solve modern problems?

Egyptology is a discipline that concerns itself with the ancient world, and thus its primary task is not to comment on contemporary problems. However, the study of ancient Egypt enables us to examine how and why culture develops and changes over the course of thousands of years. Although Egyptology deals with the ancient world, it is possible to use what we know about antiquity to analyze contemporary problems and situations. For example, in the wake of the attacks of September 11, 2001 and the wars in Iraq and Afghanistan, political interest has focused on terrorism and the alleged clash of civilizations, on globalism and the question of a more just world order, and on the possibilities of various forms of government (*e.g.*, a secular vs. a theocratic state). Ancient Egypt supplies an especially dramatic example of an analogous situation: the civil war between the Ptolemaic state under Ptolemy IV and Ptolemy V and the insurgents of the great "rebellion of the Egyptians" (207–185 BCE). This was the largest of the anti-Ptolemaic uprisings, and was directed against the economic exploitation of the rural population and the religious policy of the rulers. During this time a rival kingdom arose in the south, with Thebes as its capital, under the rulers Harwennefer and his successor, Ankhwennefer (206–186 BCE), while large parts of the Delta seceded from the government in Alexandria. Work on the temple of Edfu, a showpiece of Ptolemaic architecture, came to a halt. It was during this period that Egypt lost its foreign territorial possessions once and for all, entailing huge losses in revenue and resulting in Egypt's decline on the stage of international politics. A decade-long war of attrition finally turned the tables on the rebels.

Interestingly, central elements of the ongoing conflicts in Iraq and Afghanistan were foreshadowed in this civil war during the Ptolemaic era. The Greek historian Polybius describes the conflict as an unconventional war, involving guerilla attacks and terrorist strikes, and his account lays emphasis on the atrocities and the lawlessness of the attacks. The Ptolemaic authorities responded with state-sanctioned force, torturing and crucifying the "godless" rebel leaders of Lower Egypt. As an underlying cause of the present-day conflict, commentators have cited western globalization at the expense of a fair allocation of resources and respect for the equality of cultural values. In much the same way, Hellenism was the world's first example of the phenomenon of "globalization," and the Hellenizing of Egypt has been compared to the Americanization of Europe in the twentieth century. A moderate globalization occurred in early Ptolemaic Egypt, with the representatives of the state being the "western" representatives of new cultural developments. The new elite's economic exploitation for the sake of financing foreign policy and the stateliness of the royal court led increasingly to the impoverishment of large numbers of the native population. At the same time, the native elite were excluded from the possibility of political discourse, no doubt increasing their sense of oppression and powerlessness.

Egypt's civil war thus showcases the same alternative of either isolation or active engagement in a globalized world that we see in the modern Middle East. The constellation of the Ptolemaic civil war also posed a choice between two different models of the state, which have their parallels in the modern world. In contrast to the "secular" Graeco-Egyptian Ptolemaic state, the rebel leaders in Thebes established a radically orthodox, repressive, nationalistic theocratic state. As in our own time, bringing an end to the conflict called for a policy of reconciliation and balance. Although, in fairness, it needs to be said that the state system of Ptolemaic Egypt was the political consequence of a world that was already closely integrated, the conclusion of the civil war saw a reduction of the prerogatives of the Ptolemaic king in favor of the native Egyptian elite, a general amnesty (*inter alia*, for the police forces in rebel-held areas), a remission of debts, and a reduction in taxes that corrected earlier social imbalances.

2

The Egyptian World and the Egyptian World View

11.

Was everything entirely different in ancient Egypt?

> Just as the climate that the Egyptians have is entirely their own and different from anyone else's, and their river has a nature quite different from other rivers, so, in fact, the most of what they have made their habits and their customs are the exact opposite of other folks.

So begins the account of Egyptian customs written by the Greek historian Herodotus, who perhaps visited Egypt in about 450 BCE. Herodotus' point was to portray Egypt as an exotic world antithetic to Greek culture. Some of his examples are by and large correct—for example, circumcision, priests shaving their hair, writing from right to left, and the restriction of priestly offices to men. Others, however, are not entirely accurate: women would go shopping in the market, while men would stay home and do the weaving (though women are indeed depicted in market scenes, and we see men using vertical looms), or people would relieve themselves in their houses and eat in the streets, contrary to the custom elsewhere (well-to-do Egyptians did in fact have a sort of indoor toilet or latrine, but not most of the population; see **Question 89**). Indeed, today we would recognize some ancient Egyptian customs as familiar, while others would be either uncommon or unknown.

Yet in much the same way as Herodotus felt about his world, Egypt viewed itself as the cultural "norm" and described the lands beyond its borders as exotic and alien. Outside of Egypt the rivers ran backwards (referring to the

Euphrates, which flows from north to south), birds laid an egg every day (hens, which were presented to Thutmose III in the Lebanon), and men wore belts (the Greeks). However, through cultural exchanges every culture, including Egypt, absorbs exotic elements into its own repertoire. With regard to the domestic sphere referred to by Herodotus, one may note that an Egyptian household contained many items introduced from abroad, including glass, colored clothing (see **Question 98**), drinking straws, and—introduced by the Hittites or Hurrians in late Dynasty 18—shoes (as opposed to sandals) and socks, examples of which were found in Tutankhamun's tomb treasure (see **Question 88**). Herodotus' portrayal of Egypt as an entirely alien culture is thus as false, or, at least, oversimplified, as the modern assertion that Egypt, along with Greece and Israel, is one of the three pillars of western civilization. Both stereotypes—Egypt as an exotic and a familiar civilization—are relevant to our modern fascination with ancient Egypt, and modern observers can scarcely avoid them; they even permeate the scholarly literature. While not everything in ancient Egypt was different from today, Egyptian culture must be understood on its own terms, taking into account the continual changes it experienced over time.

 **12.**

What is in fact Egyptian about ancient Egypt?

A culture like that of ancient Egypt can be understood as a complex system of symbols that were shared and understood by the bearers of that culture. Its elements and its forms of expression included, among other things, language and religion, art and architecture, literature, and clothing, all of which were distinctly "Egyptian" in character. Thus, in ancient Egypt we find a particular vocabulary (see **Question 72**), a unique belief system (see **Questions 38, 39, 45** and **48**), special artistic conventions and architectural forms (see **Questions 41** and **53**), literary works that followed specific structures (see **Questions 74** and **75**), and distinctive clothing styles (see **Questions 16** and **98**). Elements of other symbolic systems can be recognized as deviating from the Egyptian system, referring either to another culture or to a new culture. For example, in the late fourth millennium BCE many graves exhibit a form of burial in which the corpse was not kept intact. Rather, certain body parts (such as the head or the extremities) were separated and interred apart from one another (see **Question 48**). Around 3000 BCE, however, this "rival" form of burial was excluded from the standardization of obligatory burial practices (as were divergent artistic conventions), and with that, it was no longer Egyptian. The tomb of Petosiris from the late fourth century BCE, provides an example for the inclusion of new cultural elements within the Egyptian framework. Although it was constructed in the form of an Egyptian temple, its interior scenes include Greek motifs, showing that Hellenistic elements had become a part of Egyptian culture and thus of the symbolic system that was understood by the inhabitants of Egypt.

For changes in meaning or new symbolic systems to be accepted, the essential factor was the manner in which they were introduced into the traditional culture: gradual change allowed new elements to be integrated and, in the process, to be perceived as less foreign. This point finds dramatic illustration in the new cultural doctrine of the Amarna Period, which included many elements that can be called "un-Egyptian" (see **Questions 33 and 64**). For example, the god no longer inhabited dwellings on earth, but was only able to touch the earth through his solar rays; to allow for this action to occur, the new temples of the period were unroofed, divulging their interiors; the former massive gateways (pylons) of the traditional temples became mere walls separating temple courtyards. In place of the absent god, the king was now revered; in private tombs, scenes of the royal family replaced representations of the tomb owner, and depictions of the funeral disappeared almost completely. The sun god no longer brought the deceased back to life at night in the netherworld; rather, he awakened the deceased in the narrow confines of the latter's tomb when he rose on the eastern horizon in the morning. The whole Egyptian system of religious meaning was (at least, in the new, sacred royal residence of Amarna) declared to be no longer valid and binding. It was replaced by a new system of meaning, and although it rested on Egyptian precursors and has often been praised in modern times as an intellectual—and spiritual—breakthrough, in its own time, this new system must have been viewed by most as un-Egyptian and incomprehensible.

13.

What did Egypt look like in antiquity?

Climate change and human intervention have changed Egypt more drastically since ancient times than it might at first appear. The most severe modern intervention was the construction of high dams at Aswan in Egypt (1899–1902 and 1960–1971) and at Meroe in the Sudan (2000–2009), which brought an end to an ecological system that had functioned for millennia. Direct negative consequences include significant loss of water through seepage and evaporation from the lakes created by the dams, increasing salinization of the soil, an end to the natural fertilization of the fields by the sediments that were deposited annually by the inundation, and increasing erosion of the Mediterranean coastline. Today's expanding withdrawal of water for irrigation and agriculture, combined with unchecked population growth, is likely to lead to future water shortages and major political conflicts.

The ancient Egyptians did not develop methods for controlling the waters of the Nile, leaving them at the mercy of natural climatic fluctuations. Between 15,000 and 2800 BCE a wet phase made the western desert into a savannah, and created huge lakes in what is now the Sahara Desert. The water levels and the course of the Nile were determined by the volume of the annual inundation, which was itself governed by the climate of the highlands of East Africa, by the level of the Mediterranean, and by how the river itself shaped the landscape. In the area of Khartum, for instance, around 6000–5000 BCE, the level of the Nile flood was about ten meters higher than at present, while during the Later Neolithic it was about four meters higher. In the latter period, from about 4000 to 3000 BCE, the level of the Mediterranean was also higher. For this reason, beginning around 3000 BCE cemeteries and habitation sites in the Delta were either located on high sandbanks (so-called "turtle backs") or south of the inundation area. In the second half of the third millennium, the climate of northeast Africa became extremely dry. The amount of water in the Nile declined drastically, and the level of the Mediterranean fell by about five meters between 3000 and 2000 BCE. This change to an arid climate is reflected in tomb reliefs dating to the end of the Old Kingdom, Dynasties 5 and 6, which are the last to depict desert vegetation (see **Question 30**). From the end of the Old Kingdom to Dynasty 12, the drier environment allowed settlements to be located on much lower-lying ground than in the Early Dynastic Period. It is striking to realize that when the pyramids of Egypt were built in the mid-third millennium BCE on the rocky high plateaus to the west of the Nile, those plateaus were devoid of sand. Yet by 2000 BCE, the sand of the Sahara had engulfed the pyramid fields, and still covers them today. It was not until the end of the eighth century BCE that the Nilometers of Karnak recorded a reversal of this trend. During the Ptolemaic Period, the level of the Mediterranean sank further, drying out the marshy regions of the northern Delta and enabling settlement of the area, while the Christian and Islamic eras saw yet another dry phase.

The Nile Delta formed in the course of several millennia due to the enormous amount of sediments carried by the Nile from the African highlands and deposited in this alluvial land. While the Nile Delta was divided into as many as thirty-five branches in the Ramesside Period, classical antiquity counted only seven such watercourses, and these eventually became reduced to the two branches that exist today, the Rosetta and Damietta branches. The best-known example of this phenomenon is the silting up of the lower reaches of the Pelusiac branch, which forced the rulers of Dynasty 21 to abandon the city of Pi-Ramesses and relocate their residence to Tanis on the Tanitic branch of the Nile, the closest navigable branch in the north. Unlike what we see today, the ancient Delta was not mostly flat, but rather strewn with hundreds of settlement mounds. Along the Nile valley, the river changed its course over time, too. In the Theban region, for instance, it shifted continually from west to east, so that in the New Kingdom, it flowed along the row of royal funerary temples, while today it passes by the temples of Luxor and Karnak.

In antiquity, Egypt had a much richer fauna and flora than in modern times, with agriculture, population increase, domestication of animals, and climatic factors all leading to a drastic decline in the number of species. The steady decline in types of animals is well documented, and can even be seen in the religious beliefs of the ancient Egyptians, where the presence or absence of certain animals can also serve as an indication of this phenomenon. For example, by the middle of the second millennium, at the latest, elephants, rhinoceroses, giraffes, deer, water buffaloes, monkeys, and various species of antelope and gazelle had all disappeared from Egypt. Lions survived significantly longer, while ostriches and wild donkeys were reported as late as the first half of the nineteenth century, and panthers and cheetahs survived in their natural habitat even into the twentieth century, as was also the case in Palestine. Travel accounts from the sixteenth to the eighteenth centuries often mention hippopotami residing near Damietta, and they seem to have survived there until the early nineteenth century. The name Bahra et-Timsah ("Crocodile Lake") recalls the presence of crocodiles close to the town of Ismailiya, while the ancient writer Pliny (in his *Natural History*) mentioned the Saite nome in the Delta as the principal source of hippopotami for the Roman circus games. Bird species also disappeared—for instance, golden eagles and African black eagles—though they can still be encountered in the mountain ranges of North Africa and the Sinai, and occasionally in the Red Sea mountains. Sacred ibises, crested ibises, and cormorants were observed until around 1900.

There has been a similar change in plant life. Depictions of tomb owners fishing and fowling in the papyrus thickets, or the mythic episode in which the goddess Isis protected her child Horus from Seth by hiding in the marshes and reed thickets of the Delta, indicate that Egypt was originally home to diverse vegetation that could also satisfy the requirements of a rich variety of animals. Ancient sources also testify to the existence of groves and woodlands in Egypt of the historical period. Papyrus marshes at Damietta in the Delta and at Lake Manzala were recorded as late as 1820–1821, and they can still be seen in Birket Umm Risha in the Wadi Natrun. Palaeoecological research has enabled a relatively precise reconstruction of the ancient landscape, an example being the eastern Delta region of Avaris, the capital city of the Hyksos (see also **Question 56**). Such scientific studies are indispensable for our modern understanding of ancient historical developments.

Figure 3: The god of the skies Nun raises the barque with the rejuvenated sun god (Khepri) in the form of a scarab. Book of the Dead papyrus of Anhai, *c*.1050 BCE (pBM10472)

Figure 4: A decorative plaque depicting the god of the Nile inundation, Hapy, carrying an offering table that symbolizes the fertility brought to Egypt by the annual flood. Seventh century BCE

 **14.**

Did the ancient Egyptians know that the earth and sun are round?

Greek scholarship of the fourth century BCE is usually credited with recognizing the spherical shape of the earth. At the end of the third century, Eratosthenes, who headed the Library of Alexandria, calculated that the earth's circumference was about 40,000 kilometers. He based this on observations of the difference in the position of the sun between Aswan, at Egypt's southern border, and Alexandria. Though it was possible to derive the spherical shape of the earth from observations that the ancient Egyptians certainly could have made—the perceived movement of the stars in the sky, the "sinking" of a ship at sea on the horizon, or the round shadow of the earth during a lunar eclipse—we have no proof that the ancient Egyptians understood that the earth was round. Recently it was claimed that the earth's circumference can be calculated from distances recorded in the Books of the Netherworld. These texts, which mostly come from the royal tombs of the New Kingdom, describe the journey of the sun god through the twelve hours of the night, from sunset in the west to the new sunrise in the east. If we add the distances covered during these hours, when the sun god traveled on the underside of the earth's surface, and then add the east–west stretch of Egypt traversed by the sun god in his daily course through the sky, we arrive at a quite accurate calculation of the actual circumference of the earth. This has aroused controversy as it could in fact be taken as a proof that the Egyptians were able to calculate the earth's circumference, and thus that they must have believed that the earth was spherical in shape. But this hypothesis has not been generally accepted.

Egyptian reliefs from the Amarna Period depict the sundisk with a pronounced curvature that gives the impression that a hemisphere is projecting outwards from the surface of the depiction. Scholars have always assumed that this is only a stylistic peculiarity, and not an indication that the sun is spherical in shape. Yet the shape of the sun could also have been derived through analogy with the actions of the dung beetle (scarab beetle), which forms a ball of dung in which to lay its eggs. Upon hatching, the new beetles emerge from inside the dung ball. This natural phenomenon was one that the Egyptians understood as an image of rebirth and it was incorporated into their mythology in the form of Khepri, the regenerated god of sunrise, who could be depicted as a dung beetle. In the representation that concludes the Book of Gates, Khepri as a dung beetle pushes the regenerated sun towards the place where sunrise occurs (see Figure 3; see **Question 45**). Since similar analogies between the real world and the world of the gods played an important role in Egyptian religion, the Egyptians could well have spoken of the sun as a sphere. Finally, it is striking (though not previously interpreted in this sense) that the sun "disk" is called a "golden egg" in the Coffin Texts: "O Re, who is in his golden egg (or 'who is in the form of his golden egg'), who rises from (or 'as') his sun 'disk'."

15.

Why were the Egyptians oriented towards Africa?

What was the geographical orientation of ancient Egypt? In the ancient Egyptian language, the words for "right" and "west" were identical, as were the words for "forward" and "upstream," while the north was sometimes referred to as the "rear." These facts, along with the marginal significance of the sea in Egyptian religion, show that the Egyptians oriented themselves towards the south. The few depictions that can be cited in this respect—for example, the Turin gold mine map and a representation of the world on a Dynasty 30 coffin in the Metropolitan Museum of Art in New York—show the south at the top and the north at the bottom, with the east on the left and the west on the right, contrary to our own familiar picture of the world. For the ancient Egyptians, the west was the right, and thus the good side, where the deceased were buried. This made the left, or the east, the false and hostile side, where Bedouins and foreigners dwelled.

The reason for this orientation was not an Egyptian "origin" out of Africa (see **Question 4**). Despite its north–south extension, the Nile valley was never an actual corridor for cultural connection. Rather, the orientation was based on the flow of the Nile, and the direction from which its inundation flooded Egypt every summer. This phenomenon was the indirect result of rainfall in the highlands of East Africa, an occurrence unknown to the Egyptians, and denied by the Greek historian Herodotus as unbelievable. Yet it was critical for Egypt's agricultural production, and thus for Egypt's very existence, and it must also have been an important reference point for the reckoning of time (see **Question 1**). This southern orientation is apparent very early in Egypt's development, particularly in early cult places, which display a north–south orientation and are thus aligned with the Nile River. For example, the Step Pyramid complex of the Dynasty 3 King Djoser at Saqqara has its funerary temple on the north side of the pyramid (see also **Question 55**). One dynasty later, at Maidum, Snofru was the first king to have his pyramid complex oriented east–west, corresponding to the course of the sun, with its funerary temple on the east side of the pyramid. This fact is generally viewed as an expression of the increasing importance of the sun cult. Even so, the entrance to the pyramid remained on the north side, from which the deceased king ascended to join the circumpolar stars in the northern sky, attesting to the continuing significance of the north–south orientation.

16.

What color was the
Egyptian sea?

The Egyptians called the sea—whether the Mediterranean or the Red Sea—the "Great Green" (*wadj wer*), though in reality they doubtless mostly perceived the blue shade of the water, as we do. The Sacred Lake of Abydos, which was equated with the Mediterranean, was described as "of lapis lazuli (*khesbedj*) color"—that is, blue (see **Question 41** for the text).

The physiological perception of colors is by and large identical in all human beings, and since the late 1960s eleven basic categories of color perception have been defined; these are expressed in English or German, for example, as eleven primary color designations. Yet the organization and nomenclature of the color spectrum is a culture-specific matter. Like Mesopotamia, ancient Egypt knew only four primary color terms, which we usually translate as "black," "white," "red," and "green." "Black" indicated, for instance, the black-brown mud of the Nile inundation, which gave Egypt its ancient name *Kemet*, the "Black Land." Its counterpart was *hedj*, "white," which actually meant "bright, gleaming," and was used to designate such things as the bright light of the sun. The third color term was *desher*, "red," which stood for warm colors, and, in contrast to the Black Land, gave the desert its name "Red Land," *Desheret* (this word is etymologically the same as "Sahara," which also literally means "the yellowish red [desert]"). The fourth Egyptian color term was *wadj*, "green," which stood for cold colors; the word also meant "fresh" and "yellowish green," as, for instance, in the color or quality of plants. While the Egyptian language recognized only four primary color designations, all of which also had a wide range of symbolic meanings, a much larger spectrum of colors was used in painting and in the dyeing of textiles. Five different paint colors and dyes were used in the Old Kingdom, and this expanded to nine in the polychrome painting of the New Kingdom. Brightly colored fabrics are first attested in the New Kingdom at the royal court and among the elite, but they quickly spread through all the strata of society. Indeed, the common perception that Egyptians dressed in white linen rests on depictions in temples and tombs, where white was a sign of purity, but it does not apply to everyday life (see **Question 98**). The range of this color spectrum was labeled with secondary designations, such as "blue" after the color of the lapis lazuli stone. In fact, the Egyptians were the only ancient culture to have a word for blue, and "Egyptian blue" refers to the synthetic blue pigment they created in the third millennium BCE. The introduction of the color term blue likely came from the technological ability to create both this pigment and faience objects, which had a blue-green hue due to vitrification of the glazed surface during firing. This expansion of the color terminology was surely an intra-Egyptian development, though influences from the textile industry of the Levant are likely to have played an important role.

17.

Did the Egyptians know their past?

In the Late Period, especially in the seventh and sixth centuries BCE, the elite looked to the past for their cultural identity and revived older traditions and styles in their art and intellectual expression. We refer to this phenomenon as the "archaism" of ancient Egypt: old names and titles were once again used, members of the elite had themselves depicted wearing clothing styles of the Old Kingdom, and architecture, statuary, and relief sculpture followed models from the past. Ancient religious texts, such as the Pyramid Texts of the Old Kingdom, were copied and used for tomb inscriptions and on sarcophagi, and the Book of the Dead, a guide to the netherworld for the deceased, now assumed its final, canonic form. We must not understand this archaism, as scholars once did, as reflecting a decadent Egypt no longer capable of creativity and thus forced to copy the past. Quite the contrary, the Late Period elite seem to have put the past on display because they chose to make it the reference point for their cultural identity. As Jan Assmann states, the Egyptians of that period lived "in a universe of comprehensive recollection that was overwhelmingly visible before their very eyes in the form of pyramids and mastabas, sphinxes, obelisks, and stelae, and whose every corner was chronologically and historically illuminated by annals and lists, inscriptions and depictions."

This was not an entirely new practice. Knowledge of and conscious orientation towards the past was already widespread in the literature and architecture of the Middle and New Kingdoms. Senwosret III was candidly named "a preserver of the past," and was praised as follows: "How joyful are your fathers who once lived, now that you have increased their offering portions!" Egyptian royal ideology placed the occupant of the throne in a long series of kings whose monuments he restored and to whom he made offerings; the royal ancestor cult was thus an important component of royal ideology, especially during the New Kingdom. Past kings were present in the form of statues, and their names were entered into lists, the best known of which is the King List of Sety I at Abydos. The early kings of Dynasty 18 took the Middle Kingdom as their model. Thutmose III renovated the Hypostyle Hall at Karnak, taking care that the statues of earlier kings remained easily visible, and he included a king list in his Festival Hall. Amenhotep III stressed that he had outdone his predecessors, bragging that he was the first king who once again celebrated festivals of royal renewal (*sed* festivals) "in accordance with the old writings," for "no previous generations had carried out the *Sed* festival (correctly) since the time of Re."

Political decisions were based on an exact knowledge of the immediate past. In texts such as the boundary stelae of Akhenaten or the retrospective account of Ramesses IV in Papyrus Harris, the time chronicled encompasses around seventy years. But the Egyptian court (see also **Question 94**) also endeavored to view political actions in a longer historical perspective. To find comparable situations, as we read in a text from the reign of Ramesses IV, "they searched the annals from the most ancient kings down to the time of their ancestors." The result was usually negative, thus stressing the incomparability of the king in question; hundreds of text passages testify to events that were unprecedented and unique. Thus, it was declared of the conquests of Thutmose I that such deeds "could not be found in the annals of the predecessors since the Followers of Horus"—that is, the kings of the first dynasties. The vizier Rekhmire said of Thutmose III, "Truly, his majesty knew history/what happened"; indeed, this king allegedly steeped himself in texts from the reign of Khufu, a thousand years in the past. The Ramesside kings engaged in an even more distinct reverence for their ancestors and antiquity. Khaemwese, the fourth son of Ramesses II, restored royal pyramids of the Old Kingdom in Saqqara. Ramesses II examined ancient writings regarding the origins and the theological importance of Thebes; Merneptah consulted them when Egypt was threatened by Libyans (see **Question 35**); Ramesses IV searched them for historical parallels to a miracle that occurred in his reign. Even in cases like these, however, history was never pursued out of pure scholarly interest, but rather for the purpose of legitimizing political measures (see **Question 76**).

 **18.**

Did the Egyptians explore the world?

In his "Histories," the Greek father of historiography, Herodotus, gives an account of the first circumnavigation of Africa (called "Libya" in Herodotus' account), allegedly commissioned by the Egyptian King Nekho II and executed by Phoenician sailors around 600 BCE. The crew would have departed from the Red Sea, and returned home at the beginning of the third year of their journey. Herodotus says (and this could be an indicator of the veracity of the account): "On their return, they declared—I for my part do not believe them, but perhaps others may—that in sailing round Libya they had the sun upon their right hand." While there is no proof so far that this expedition actually happened, there is ample evidence that the Egyptians embarked on long-distance travel as early as the Old Kingdom. Recent excavations on the Red Sea coast have not only uncovered shipbuilding and harbor installations of the Middle Kingdom but also revealed extensive port installations from the Pyramid Age (around 2500 BCE). These gave the Egyptians the ability to sail the Red Sea and probably establish a trade-link with the country of Punt, which was located further to the south on the African coast, and was a provider of frankincense and other indigenous products. In inscriptions of the same time period, we are told that pygmies from the land of the horizon-dwellers (probably East Central Africa) were brought to the Egyptian court. The recent discovery of a desert trail leading hundreds of kilometers onto the Sahara plateau, with Egyptian rock inscriptions along it, has strengthened the hypothesis of a trade route into the Chad basin of Central

Africa where there existed a gigantic palaeolake of the size of the Caspian Sea throughout the third millennium. In the second millennium, military campaigns reached places as far as Southeast Anatolia, Cyprus, and the Euphrates River near Carchemish. It is striking to note that almost all Egyptian fictional literature from the second millennium, the time of the Middle and New Kingdoms, has an exotic setting abroad—in the Levant, Mesopotamia, or the Red Sea. Their protagonists encounter foreign realities as fugitives or castaways (Sinuhe, the Doomed Prince, the Shipwrecked Sailor; see **Question 75**).

Ancient Egyptian exploration of foreign countries was not normally undertaken for the sake of discovery and knowledge, but was rather a side-product of economic and military purposes. The desire to know and understand the variety and nature of the created world may, however, have been a pivotal element in the decoration of the so-called "Botanical Garden" of Thutmose III (see **Question 41**). This sanctuary within the temple of Karnak contains a meticulous display of exotic animals and plants from across the Near East and Africa, and of extraordinary species from Egypt, demonstrating that Amun is the generator of life in all its forms and aspects. If, as has been proposed, this sanctuary also served as a place of initiation for the priests, then the building's revelation of the richness of life and the techniques of Amun's creation can also be seen as a repertoire of knowledge for the very sake of knowledge.

 # 19.

Can we explain ancient Egypt's culture through its landscape?

In 1887 the historian George Rawlinson described Egypt as a place where cultural achievements occurred as a result of, and a reaction to, the allegedly monotonous landscape. In Rawlinson's view the Egyptians created mighty construction works in deliberate contrast to the boredom of the natural setting. For Walther Wolf (1938) it was, quite to the contrary, the great expanse of the land that was the very reason for the monumentality of architecture. He saw evidence for the Egyptians' well-developed sense of color and form in the sharp color contrast between Nile and desert, the basis for their strong feel for line in the form of the Nile valley, and the ultimate cause for their seriousness in the supposedly unromantic character of the landscape.

Though such explanations are often subjective and fail to account for either the variety of phenomena or for changes over time (see **Question 13**), Egypt's landscape and climate were nevertheless the framework for its history. From Egypt's environment we can derive more than just the time and place of its settlement, its economic productivity, and the historical alternation of periods of unity and political division. Religious phenomena such as the existence and nature of certain deities, the conduct of festivals, and mythological concepts, were also directly shaped by the nature of the land. At Abydos, for instance, the royal tombs of the Early Dynastic Period lie at the mouth of a valley that leads into the western desert and, although not yet archaeologically explored, could provide an explanation for the location of the cemetery at this spot. At Egypt's southern border, on the island of Elephantine, where the Nile inundation (Figure 4) entered into Egypt, the cults of the cataract deities Satis, Anukis, and Khnum (an important creator god) were closely connected with the natural setting and can be archaeologically traced over the course of more than three millennia. At Mendes in the Nile Delta, religious and intellectual development—from the original dolphin goddess Hatmehit, via the fertility cult of the Ram of Mendes, to the perfume industry of classical antiquity, the natural philosopher Bolos of Mendes, and the decline of the city— can be understood only against the background of its natural setting. Although able to enrich our understanding of ancient Egypt, such attempts at interpretation, however, are seldom systematically undertaken by Egyptologists.

 **20.**

What is the "great unknown" of Egyptian civilization?

In his inaugural lecture at the Collège de France in 1961, the French Egyptologist Georges Posener spoke at length of what we do not know about Egypt, of the immeasurable loss of historical information. The focus of his remarks was what he called the "great unknown" of Egyptian culture: the area of Lower Egypt—the huge alluvial expanse of the Nile Delta between Memphis, south of modern Cairo, and the Mediterranean coast. With its approximately 22,000 square kilometers, it has twice the area of the entire Nile valley all the way to the First Cataract at Elephantine. Until the 1970s, the Delta was little more than a big blank spot on the Egyptological map. All accounts of Egyptian civilization were by and large confined to developments in the culture of the Nile valley between Memphis and Aswan. This situation has not substantially changed, despite the fact that new surveys and excavations have been carried out in the last 40 years (see **Question 56**). Our ignorance stands in sharp contrast to the importance of Lower Egypt in the self-perception of ancient Egypt: as one of two equal parts that were united at the formation of the ancient Egyptian state, with the king as guarantor of the land's continued unity (see **Question 21**). Now, modern Egyptology pins its hopes on the Delta. Lower Egypt has variously been seen as the "cradle of Egyptian civilization," as a trailblazer for political and economic relations with foreign lands, even as the key to the solution of major problems in Egyptology.

The main reason why our knowledge of this part of Egypt is so limited is that it represents the most extreme case of loss of evidence. From 6000 BCE on, the annual Nile floods, which ceased only with the construction of the modern dams at Aswan, did more than just create the Delta as a geographical feature with its deposits of alluvial soil (see **Question 13**). They also covered the ancient habitation sites of Lower Egypt with several meters of sediment layers. Still more alarming are the human encroachments of the nineteenth and twentieth centuries, which have entailed the removal or overbuilding of most of the previously intact tells (ruin mounds) of ancient settlements. The most impressive—and distressing—example is that of Sais, an ancient royal capital in the western Delta. In 1828, its colossal ruins, which still stood to a height of 25 meters, looked to Jean-François Champollion like the remains of a palace erected by giants. Today, there is nothing left to see; since the beginning of the twentieth century, its ruins have disappeared, like those of hundreds of other cities and towns. The situation has also been exacerbated by ongoing demographic developments. Only four percent of the area of modern Egypt is useful for habitation and agriculture, and since the beginning of the twentieth century, the population of these 35,000 square kilometers has increased tenfold to more than 80 million.

Egypt represents an archaeological disaster area. The Egyptian Ministry of Agriculture releases "uninteresting" ancient habitation sites for settlement by the ever-increasing population, and, now that the alluvial soil once carried by the Nile floods is contained in the lake created by the High Dam at Aswan, ancient mud brick walls have been dismantled and used as building materials for modern houses or as fertilizer for the fields. Obviously, had nineteenth- and early twentieth-century Egyptologists set themselves different priorities and directed their interests to (superficially less exciting) Lower Egypt, our picture of ancient Egypt would be quite different today. Only more recently has the Egyptian Antiquities Service formally recognized the urgency of archaeological investigation in the Delta (see **Questions 8 and 56**).

# 21.

Why was the ancient Egyptian king called "King of Upper and Lower Egypt"?

The King of Egypt (Figure 5) was, at one and the same time, "King of Upper Egypt and King of Lower Egypt" (pronounced *insibya*, *c.*1300 BCE) and "Lord of the Two Lands." These double titles reflect the ancient Egyptian king's rule over both the Nile valley, beginning at the first cataract in Elephantine, and the Delta region. Correspondingly, the country's administration was (at least formally) divided into two parts, and each part of the land had its own symbol, its own protective deity, and its own institutions (including "national" sanctuaries). The primordial capitals of the two parts of the land were understood to be Buto in the Delta, with its goddess Wadjit, patron goddess of Lower Egypt, and Hierakonpolis in Upper Egypt, whose protective deity was Nekhbet, goddess of the town of el-Kab, which was situated across the river from Hierakonpolis. In mythology, the two gods Horus and Seth, who battled over the kingship of Egypt, also reflected the land's division into two parts (Figure 6).

In the fourth millennium, the Buto and Maadi cultures represented the characteristic regional culture in the Delta. They functioned as the hub for the international trade with western Asia, and indicators of these trade connections within the Buto-Maadi-culture include the use of copper in the manufacture of weapons and tools, and "pit" houses whose floors were sunk below ground level. Both phenomena are known from contemporary Palestine, attesting to the close interaction between the two areas. While Lower Egypt served as the conduit through which western Asian goods and technological innovations flowed into the south, Upper Egypt was the way station for trade goods from Nubia and the Sudan. Southern luxury items, such as cosmetic palettes, were imitated in the north. In the culture of Buto and Maadi, we believe there existed specialized occupations, social stratification, and a rudimentary writing system for the registration of goods— although the latter is as yet attested in Upper Egypt only at Abydos, around 3250 BCE (see **Question 71**). The cultural autonomy of the Delta can be seen in ceramics and the flint industry, as well as in burial customs, where, in contrast to the Naqada culture of Upper Egypt, the faces of the deceased were oriented to the east rather than the west. Between 3300 and 3200 BCE, Upper Egyptian Naqada ceramics, previously unattested in the Delta, completely replaced the ceramics of Lower Egypt. However, burial customs remained the same, indicating that the new ceramic forms were adopted by the Lower Egyptians and that there was no radical change in the population of the Delta.

Although earlier generations of scholars assumed a military conquest of the Delta by the south around 3000 BCE, as supposedly illustrated by the famous palette of King Narmer, Egypt seems rather to have been culturally—but not necessarily politically—united as early as 3200 BCE (see **Question 23**). Between 3300 and 3200 BCE, the material culture of both Lower and Upper Egypt underwent changes, pointing to the fact that this was a time when significant transformations in culture occurred throughout the entire country. The two parts of the land seem to have had kingships of their own prior to the pan-Egyptian Dynasty 1. Kings of the so-called "Dynasty 0" are known from their tombs and enclosures at Abydos in Upper Egypt, while rulers of Lower Egypt are indicated in the king list on the Palermo Stone (so-called after the city in Sicily where the stone slab is now on display). In artistic representations from before and after the founding of Dynasty 1, the king appears as ruler of both parts of the land, wearing the distinctive crowns of Upper Egypt and Lower Egypt, yet Lower Egypt is clearly depicted as vanquished and inferior in status. Political conflicts between the two parts of the land and frequent political divisions are attested down through Dynasty 2. An oft-depicted ideological scene, the "Uniting of the Two Lands," points to the unstable nature of the united kingdom, which was always apt to break up into separate realms.

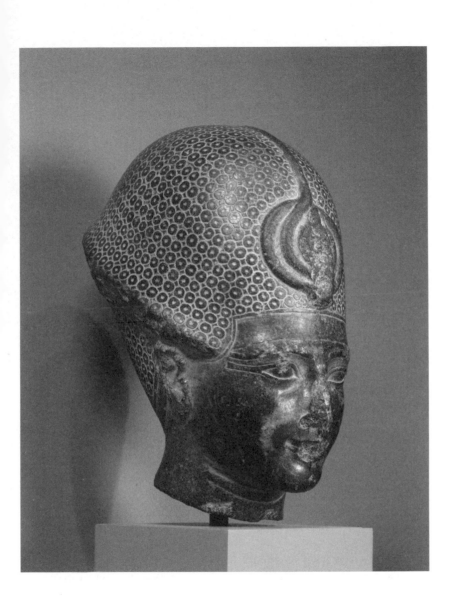

Figure 5: Head of a statue of Amenophis III (*c.*1370 BCE), recarved for Ramesses II (*c.*1270 BCE). The King wears the Blue or War Crown with a protective Uraeus serpent at its front.

22.

Was ancient Egypt a culture of death?

In his novel *Joseph and His Brothers*, Thomas Mann called Egypt the "realm of death," and the land where death was worshipped. The Egyptologist Jan Assmann has recently described death as "the center of the consciousness" and the generator of Egyptian culture. In the face of an average life expectancy of only around thirty years and a high rate of infant mortality, the prospect of death loomed closer in the life of the individual than it does today. Egyptian royalty and elites expended a considerable part of their resources and incomes on overcoming death and securing their lives in the hereafter. But the modern observer runs the risk of being misled by the lopsided nature of the evidence, which is caused by the unequal distribution of preserved objects between the desert and the cultivable land. Cemeteries, for instance, were located mostly on the western desert plateau, where topography and climate favored their preservation, while habitation remains, located in the depression of the Nile valley, and especially its mud-brick buildings, have largely perished. Settlements—including whole capital cities such as Memphis, with their palaces, industrial quarters, harbors, garrisons, and all the places where Egypt's population of several million people spent their lives—are almost entirely lost or lie unexcavated (see also **Question 20**). The monuments, objects, and writings preserved to us from ancient Egypt are thus overwhelmingly tombs, tomb furnishings, and funerary texts.

Today, our picture of ancient Egypt is disproportionate to what it was originally and thus dramatically distorted.

Figure 6: Upper part of the funerary stela of King Wadj that marked the place of his royal tomb at Abydos. The serpent hieroglyph inscribed in the palace facade is a writing of the King's name. The horus falcon above the façade means the presence inside the palace of the King, who was the successor of Egypt's mythological first king, the god Horus.

To illustrate how much has been lost, I cite an example supplied by Georges Posener: of the written records produced in the Dynasty 5 funerary temple of King Neferirkare at Abusir during the eighty years of its existence, which we may assume amounted to approximately 10,000 meters in length, we have merely thirteen meters. We have a similar amount from the temple chancery of Illahun, to which can be added the recently discovered papyri from the funerary temple of Reneferef at Abusir. This is the entirety of what is left to us of the papyrus documents from all the temples of ancient Egypt. We thus have perhaps one thousandth of all the documents once produced by the three temples just mentioned! But in Egypt there were always hundreds of temples, many of them more important than these three, and from periods when huge numbers of documents were produced. How many kilometers-worth of documents, none of them preserved to us, would have been produced every year just in the great Theban temples of the New Kingdom? We would be optimistic if we estimated—as Posener did—that we have one millionth of all the documents ever written in Egyptian temples. And that estimate is confined only to the temples; it does not take into account the records of the municipal administrations and the courts, or documents stemming from transactions between private persons. It is clear that if we had balanced documentation, including the millions of secular documents produced in capital cities, death and funerary monuments would no longer appear as the center of cultural consciousness.

Since most of the ancient population was too poor to make lavish provisions for life in the hereafter (see **Question 88**), it is plausible that there were other areas of focus in the lives of individuals, families, and society. We must also make mention of a growing crisis in the beliefs about the afterlife. For example, in the autobiography of Taimhotep, who died in 42 BCE, we read,

The west, it is a land of sleep,
Darkness weighs on the dwelling-place,
Those who are there sleep in their mummy-forms.

They wake not to see their brothers,
They see not their fathers, their mothers,
Their hearts forgot their wives, their children.
The water of life which has food for all,
It is thirst for me (. . .)
As for death, "Come!" is his name,
All those that he calls to him
Come to him immediately,
Their hearts afraid through dread of him.

This Taimhotep, who called upon those who read her inscription to take pleasure in their lifetimes on earth, was the wife of the high priest of Ptah in Memphis under Cleopatra VII. Her lament over death and the afterlife thus reflects the prevailing opinion of the Egyptian elite at that time.

3

Egyptian History

 **23.**

When did ancient Egypt's history begin?

From the ancient Egyptian point of view, Egypt became a civilization around 3000 BCE through an inaugural act: the so-called "uniting of the Two Lands" (see **Question 21**). Earlier scholars saw this supposedly military unification—the conquest of Lower Egypt by Upper Egypt—reflected on contemporary decorated palettes and (ritually used) mace heads bearing depictions of the Upper Egyptian ruler smiting the inhabitants of Lower Egypt. Until the middle of the twentieth century, Egypt was viewed as a civilization that made its appearance as a high culture, as though out of nothing, around 3000 BCE. It was at times thought that a so-called "dynastic race" was responsible for the introduction of civilization to the Nile valley. Since the 1960s, however, new excavations have greatly increased our archaeological and (for the period around 3000 BCE) textual evidence, making prehistory (or Predynastic) and Early Dynastic (also called Archaic) history into specialized fields in which major radical changes have occurred.

The transition from (so-called) prehistory to history is usually set at this time, the turn of the fourth to the third millennium. The argument underlying this division is that prehistory encompasses the stages leading up to a given civilization, and that the Egyptian character of ancient Egyptian civilization (see **Question 12**) was only achieved at the time of Dynasty 1—with the establishment of the institution of kingship, territorial integrity, and a culture that can overall be called "Egyptian." The invention of writing is also part of the traditional criterion used to distinguish between prehistory and history: a past documented by written records is usually regarded as "history." This division at the beginning of Dynasty 1 is not unproblematic, however, as Egyptian culture seems to have been relatively united a good two hundred years earlier, around 3200 BCE (see **Question 21**), while the discovery of early texts on labels and jar inscriptions from Abydos has also pushed the appearance of writing in Egypt back by about a quarter of a millennium (see **Question 71**). On the other hand, we have scarcely any written historical sources, in the stricter sense of the term, from even half a millennium later, *c.*2500 BCE. Moreover, there are cultural phenomena that Early Dynastic Egypt shared with the preceding Predynastic Period, but not with the subsequent Old Kingdom and succeeding periods—for example, the exclusive use of the Horus name by kings, decorated palettes, and cylinder seals. Should the Early Dynastic Period therefore not be counted as part of historical Egypt?

If we view "historical" Egypt as the product of a gradual development, its characteristics must have taken form over a long period of time in the regional cultures of the fifth and fourth millennia. The histories of these cultures should not, however, be viewed and evaluated just from the standpoint of the later Egyptian state—that is, as constituting its prehistory— but as historical epochs in their own right. In this regard, excavations conducted since the 1970s in Egypt's western and eastern deserts have considerably broadened the horizon of our understanding. One example is the site of Nabta Playa, some 100 kilometers west of Abu Simbel and accidentally discovered in 1974. It has proved to be an important ceremonial center of the Neolithic era where, between 5500 and 3500 BCE, complex cultic structures were erected, including a stone circle marking the summer solstice, cattle burials in individual tomb chambers, and puzzling structures of as-yet unclear function, with hewn megaliths placed below the surface. The excavators expressed the opinion that Nabta Playa could have been a place where agriculturalists from the Nile valley gathered together with cattle nomads of the eastern Sahara, thus contributing to the social and religious development of early Egypt. This

contribution is also evident in the case of the Badari culture
(5000–3800 BCE), attested by more than six hundred tombs and
forty settlements in Middle Egypt, and maybe also indigenous
to the eastern (at that time) savanna and throughout the
mountains to the Red Sea coast. The statuettes and pottery
decoration of this culture present us with an incredibly rich
symbolic universe. Though there is debate as to whether rock
drawings of the eastern desert can be ascribed to this Badari
culture, and if so, whether they represent the "missing link"
that explains the emergence of ancient Egyptian civilization, it
remains certain that without Badari we cannot understand the
later, historical Egypt.

Following the Badari culture, how did the nuclei of later
political power and the Egyptian state develop? At the end
of the fourth millennium, progressive desertification of the
Sahara (see **Question 13**) forced cattle-breeding groups into the
Nile valley, where agriculture and irrigation were determining
factors. In certain communities, possession of agriculturally
useful land must have increased, and with it, the demand
for more land, so that finally these communities developed
into regional agricultural centers, and ultimately into cities
or city-states that controlled transregional importation of
building materials and luxury goods considered necessary by
emerging elites. With the appearance of social differentiation,
there arose a class of persons who supervised the production
of sustenance for the population. Luxury goods, writing and
art, material preparations for the afterlife, and a common
ideology endowed the ruling elite with a sense of identity
that contributed to the development of what we recognize
as ancient Egyptian civilization, and thus the beginning of
ancient Egypt's "history."

 **24.**

When did ancient Egypt end?

Most accounts of Egyptian history end with Alexander the Great's conquest of Egypt in 332 BCE, or with the end of the Ptolemaic dynasty in 30 BCE. Egyptologists often claim, citing various reasons, that including the new historical epoch that began with the Hellenistic era or with Roman rule over the land of the Nile is no longer necessary. But is this really true? When did the history of ancient Egypt end? The narrow criteria of "national independence" and "existence of the most classic possible Egyptian culture" to define what was truly ancient Egyptian can no longer withstand a critical glance from our contemporary standpoint. Comparatively speaking, Egypt was in many respects stamped by foreign influences as much during the first millennium before the Hellenistic era as it was in the millennium after Alexander, so that the division is largely artificial. From the Graeco-Roman era stem not only some of Egypt's largest preserved temples, with their compilations of religious and cultural knowledge (see **Question 55**), but also the principal works of Demotic literature (see also **Question 81**). The ideology of Egyptian kingship remained in force after 332 BCE, as did certain policies of state and types of cultural expression. It was also in this period that Egyptian religion exerted a previously undreamt-of influence throughout the Mediterranean world, though in a special, Egyptianizing form (see **Question 7**), remaining one of the important voices in the debates involving Christianity, Gnosis, Manichaeism, and Neoplatonism.

For these reasons, the French historians Bertrand Lançon and Christian-Georges Schwentzel have—probably correctly—proposed an entirely different end point for ancient Egypt's history, the end of the fourth century CE, when two symbols of Egyptian culture disappeared. At this time the Serapeum of Alexandria, sanctuary of the Apis bull, was destroyed and the precise location of Alexander the Great's tomb in Alexandria was supposedly forgotten. The adoption of Christianity and wide-ranging administrative reforms are also widely seen as marking the transition of Egypt from the Roman to the Christian-Byzantine world. The late fourth century CE was, moreover, when the ancient Egyptian writing system ceased to be used (see **Question 68**), spelling the end of a millennia-old tradition and thus the cultural identity of Egypt. It is in this context that the famous Apocalypse of Asclepius, a text that might indeed have been written at the end of the fourth century, paints a dismal picture of the irretrievable loss of ancient Egyptian culture (see **Question 37** for the text). In Late Antiquity, this loss of knowledge of the old writing system accelerated the mystification of ancient Egypt: incomprehensible Egypt now became a culture of mystery (see Preface). It is this point in time, when Egypt's living cultural tradition came to a definitive end, which should thus be taken as the genuine finale of ancient Egypt.

25.

Can we know what really happened in ancient Egypt?

The past is not directly accessible to us, but is preserved in the form of highly fragmentary and unbalanced historical sources. This means that we must reconstruct it through our questions and interpretations, and it also means that our knowledge is limited and often hypothetical. What do we really want to know about ancient Egypt? And what do we understand by "history"? Many factors, both conscious and unconscious, influence the questions and interpretations of historians: their own education and personal life experience, as well as their cultural background, *Zeitgeist*, the political situation, and so forth. The historical researcher and the times in which he or she lives are thus determining factors in our reconstruction of the past. As the famous ancient historian Eduard Meyer once wrote, "at all times, the understanding of history that we can achieve is always our own, it is never absolute and unconditional."

Most reconstructions of Egyptian history begin with the implicit assumption that all relevant information is known to us—if not quantitatively (much has been lost), then qualitatively (nothing essential has been lost). But our sources stem overwhelmingly from the funerary realm (temples and tombs; see also **Question 22**), from the Nile valley, and from the elite. Largely missing are the majority of society, Lower Egypt, and the large cities with their residential areas, palaces, and industrial quarters (see **Questions 56 and 96**). What is available thus is in the right, and what is absent is in the wrong (Arnold

Esch). There is also the problem of Egyptologists' uncritical use of sources, with many modern "histories" merely parroting texts commissioned by Egyptian kings. But these texts are committed to ideology and project an ideal understanding of history; they do not yield a correct and balanced picture of the past (see **Question 76**). Reconstructing the past requires one to move forward in unknown terrain, with the destination hidden from view—a balancing act between the fragmentary evidence, the multiplicity of possible interpretations of the sources, and the ultimate comprehensive description.

26.

What do we still not know about ancient Egypt?

New finds and findings show that whole areas of Egyptian culture have been unknown to us, and no doubt many more await discovery. For example, inscriptions of Dynasty 4 kings along a desert road leading far into the Sahara from el-Kharga Oasis and a new inscription of Mentuhotep II (Dynasty 11) at Gebel Uweinat, 700 kilometers from Thebes, bear witness to Old Kingdom trade activity in the Sahara and forays into the Lake Chad area of North-Central Africa at an earlier date than had once seemed likely. The recently discovered remains of the workers who built Akhenaten's new capital city of Amarna on the soil of Middle Egypt indicate hard physical labor and malnutrition, thus challenging the often idealized modern image of Amarna. In recent years, the publication of thousands of Graeco-Roman-era texts in the Demotic script and language has necessitated that we reconsider our picture of many aspects of Egyptian religion and literature (see also **Questions 70** and **81**). There is also the difficulty of determining the actual antiquity of ideas from preserved manuscripts which are often preserved hundreds of years after we need to assume the original text must have been written. These examples show the extent to which our knowledge is dependent on the number and the kind of material and textual evidence that has been preserved to us. We have already seen (**Questions 20** and **22**) that the mundane sector and Lower Egypt—whole areas of ancient Egypt—are scantily preserved or have received little archaeological attention.

The accident of preservation also has a social aspect. Who, after all, were in a position to leave evidence of their lives for posterity? It is obvious that our knowledge of ancient Egyptians is almost exclusively restricted to the royal court and the upper stratum of society. For example, the land register of Papyrus Wilbour from the reign of Ramesses V mentions fishermen, farmers, water carriers, and the like, but for administrative purposes. Thus, while the document at least makes us aware of the existence of such ordinary Egyptians, it does not enlighten their historical, individual lives. We derive limited insights from legal proceedings and police investigations—for example, the tomb robbery lawsuits of late Dynasty 20—but these are cases that fall outside the norm. On the whole, only the upper class left evidence about themselves, while accounts of the lives of ordinary Egyptians belong to the "category of never written sources" (Arnold Esch; see **Question 96**). A well-known exception is the village of Deir el-Medina, home to the men who worked on the royal tombs on the west bank of Thebes, and whose everyday lives are attested to us through thousands of documents (see also **Question 43**). This is not a representative town, however, but rather a privileged social group of artisans. Even so, we have for once some evidence of the real lives of individuals, such as the reasons for absence from work ("a scorpion stung him") or the inglorious moral conduct of the foreman Paneb, who is more known to us than the pharaoh he served. Usually, however, the evidence privileges the elite, and men are better documented than women (though we have some autobiographies of women, see **Questions 22 and 92**). We recognize the accident of preservation when it reveals such persons from the shadow side of the documentation: wet-nurses, dancing women, mouse trappers and the like who are mentioned on expired Hellenistic-era contracts that were recycled as material for mummification.

But even events are subject to a lopsided chance of preservation, for negative events produce more written evidence than positive ones. It would be a mistake to draw conclusions regarding the wretchedness of an epoch from nothing more than an abundance of preserved records of complaints and legal proceedings (as has been done for the late Ramesside Period). The era might have seen a far greater number of conflict-free lives that did not yield such documentation, or nuisances might have been tackled much more energetically during a particular period than previously (and thus left more records). Here is an example of an erroneous conclusion derived from preserved evidence: from the absence of weapons among the grave goods of a cemetery at Minshat Abu Omar, scholars concluded that this Predynastic and Early Dynastic Period settlement had no military function. This interpretation, however, is not valid. The burial customs prevailing at that time did not include the placing of weapons in tombs, and thus their absence says nothing about the military character of the settlement.

The accident of preservation also depends on the genres of the texts in question. We have only *one* king list on papyrus, only *one* New Kingdom land register, only *one* copy of the Memphite Theology (which was preserved only because it was used as a foundation to a column in Graeco-Roman times!), and so forth. In the case of literary works, their preservation depended especially on whether or not they were regarded as "classics" and entered the curriculum of scribal education (see **Questions 75** and **78**). And as for the written sources of the royal court and the elite, ideological considerations determined what should or should not be recorded. Negative events—defeats on the battlefield or illnesses—were therefore seldom included in the sources, so as not to preserve their memory forever and give them a magical reality (see **Question 76**).

Figure 7: House altar of the Amarna period, depicting Akhenaten, his wife Nefertiti and their first three daughters seated in the light of their god Aten, shown as a sundisk with rays giving life to the royal family

27.

Could Egyptian history have followed a different course?

At any given time, history can presumably take a different course, provided we do not assume that its path is determined or preordained—for instance, by divine authority. Historians must consider possible developments that were in a seminal state but did not become reality—that is, they must inquire after the "history that did not happen," but which could have resulted from the circumstances and patterns of an epoch. How differently we imagine the course of history depends essentially on how much stress we place on the various factors that contribute to historical development: the individual, society, and long-term conditions. The simplest conceivable manipulation is on the level of short-term political history—a later date for the death of a king, or the assumption of a military victory instead of the defeat that actually occurred. Longer-term social, economic, or religious changes—for instance, the increase in "personal piety" during the second millennium BCE or the rise of animal worship and oracular practices—have complex causes and might have occurred even if political history had taken a different course. But there are also long-term phenomena that could not have been different, even in alternative scenarios for Egyptian history: for example, the progressive desertification of the eastern Sahara down to about 2200 BCE (see **Question 13**), or the transition from the Bronze Age to the Iron Age between 1200 and 1000 BCE (see **Question 28**).

Only seldom and unsystematically have Egyptologists considered such alternative developments, an example being the Amarna Period (see **Question 33**): is it possible that it would not have occurred if Akhenaten's older brother had not died prematurely? This suggestion assumes that Akhenaten's historical personality was responsible for the Amarna Period, and that it was not primarily a reaction to a political or existential crisis (otherwise, this crisis might have entailed the Amarna Age anyway). Would there have been no New Kingdom, had a new Theban ruling family not assumed power around 1570 BCE and put an end to Hyksos sovereignty? Or, since conditions in the Near East after 1500 BCE caused the rise of territorial states in all the regions of the area (see **Question 32**), would there have been a different sort of New Kingdom? Would the placing of a Hittite prince on the Egyptian throne, as intended by Tutankhamun's widow around 1330 BCE, have resulted in a combined Egypto-Hittite Empire and thus prevented the Ramesside Period from occurring? A recently published cuneiform text in fact plays with the notion that Darius III defeated Alexander the Great, thus putting a stop to the Hellenization of the Near East.

Imagining alternative histories can lead to a better understanding of historical epochs because it causes the historian to examine the past from the one trajectory that was realized as the past's future—out of many possible trajectories that history could have taken but did not. Our opinion of the end of the Old Kingdom is shaped by the First Intermediate Period, and we view Amenhotep III in the light of the Amarna Period that followed his reign. We search for precursors of religious concepts that predominated under Akhenaten in what we logically call the pre-Amarna era—though it would be equally correct to do so, no Egyptologist speaks of the "post-Tuthmosid era"! Yet, in the period around 1400 BCE, Amarna was only one of several possible developments, perhaps even the least likely one.

 # 28.

What was the most decisive turning point in Egyptian history?

Was there an important discontinuity in Egyptian history, a genuine threshold between epochs? There have been, in fact, various proposals: the Hyksos Period (*c.*1600 BCE), the imperialistic foreign policy of Thutmose III (*c.*1450 BCE), the transition from Dynasty 18 to the Ramesside Period (*c.*1300 BCE), and the end of the New Kingdom, which corresponded to the transition from the Bronze Age to the Iron Age in the Near East (*c.*1100 BCE). All of these are associated with the New Kingdom, suggesting a discontinuity between an earlier and a later Egypt, both of similar chronological length. But is this really valid? The Hyksos Period is often considered the catalyst for the New Kingdom's imperial policies (see **Question 32**), as marking a radical change to an outwardly directed Egypt. However, the Middle Kingdom kings already had established a colony in Nubia and were active in the Levant. Moreover, the New Kingdom is just one of the many empires that arose around 1500 BCE across the Near East (where there were no Hyksos). The proposal of a turning point around 1450 BCE is even more biased towards foreign policy, and finds no support in the overall cultural character of the period. The Amarna Period was long suspected of having put an end to Egyptian culture; as Wolfgang Helck (wrongly!) put it: "After the death blow dealt by Amarna, Egypt was spiritually drained of blood, until nothing remained but a lifeless mummy that, admired in awe, crumbled into dust." But it is evident that many religious and cultural innovations of the Ramesside Period—for instance, a turning to the divine in so-called "personal piety," and the acknowledgement of a deity who guided the destiny of the world—can be traced back, through earlier stages, over a period of many centuries. A more decisive turning point was the demise of all the ancient Near Eastern territorial states around 1100 BCE. In Egypt, there emerged at first two power centers (one a Theban theocracy), and then a multiplicity of small states (see **Question 35**). We can ascertain a number of cultural breaks—for instance, in the ideology of kingship, tomb architecture, and literature.

But earlier historical discontinuities seem equally worthy of discussion, especially the end of the Old Kingdom. To begin with, this was the beginning of a climatic dry phase that lasted into the Ptolemaic Period. At the same time, the institution of kingship sank from an almost divine omnipotence into near total meaninglessness—in the succeeding First Intermediate Period, a provincial governor boasted, "I am the beginning and the end of mankind!" Starting in the Middle Kingdom, the gods were seen as superior to the king, and they determined history. At the end of the Old Kingdom, a new god, Osiris, gained prominence, thenceforth dominating Egyptian belief in the hereafter, while the god of kingship Horus was incorporated into the Osiris circle. In the early Middle Kingdom, another new god, Amun, began his rise to one of the most prominent positions in the pantheon. It was in the First Intermediate Period and the Middle Kingdom that Egyptian culture and literature assumed their classical forms (see **Question 31**). It might thus be legitimate to speak of two major discontinuities in Egyptian history: the end of the Old Kingdom and the end of the New Kingdom (see **Questions 30 and 35**).

 **29.**

Do we know how the ancient Egyptian economy functioned?

One of the most difficult questions regarding ancient Egypt concerns its economy. By ancient Egypt's economy we mean the institutions and mechanisms that sustained Egyptian society and provided it with resources, manufactured commodities, labour, income, and services. The economy is commonly categorized by distinguishing a primary sector (devoted to subsistence activities such as agriculture) from a secondary (processing materials and manufacturing goods) and tertiary sector (services such as transport). While we possess considerable knowledge of individual aspects of the ancient Egyptian economy, such as agriculture, manufacturing, distribution of commodities, or trade, we lack for most periods comprehensive quantitative data, and the records we have are extremely fragmentary in nature. Hardly anything, to give one example, has been preserved from the thousands of kilometers of economic records on papyri produced in temples, towns, the court, and private households (see **Question 22**). At the same time, scholars have introduced different modern economic theories into the debate, such as Keynesian economics (emphasizing the role that the ancient Egyptian state—the king—played in production and employment). However, there is an ongoing controversy surrounding the idea of an Egyptian state that would have dominated control of the economy, incurring taxes and redistributing commodities, versus the existence of a private market that creates demand and sets prices. Others have followed the example of Karl Polanyi who argued that economy is not an independent mechanism but, rather, is embedded in a given society and culture, and that therefore any economy must itself be studied as a phenomenon of society and culture.

The most important element for ancient Egypt's subsistence was its agriculture, and the economy was mainly a peasant economy. Tenant farmers produced as their main crops emmer wheat (a variety of wheat no longer cultivated very widely nowadays) and barley (for the Egyptian diet, see **Question 97**). Thus, most of Egypt's land was used for growing grain crops, and a lesser part of the country for the cultivation of vegetables, fruit trees, fodder for animals, and flax. This continued from Pharaonic through Roman times, when Egypt was Rome's breadbasket, supplying it with enormous quantities of grain every year. Apart from the agriculture, another important element of the primary sector was livestock breeding, supplemented by hunting, fishing and fowling.

Land could be owned by state institutions (such as the treasury), temples, and wealthy private individuals. Compulsory labor, rather than true slavery, seems to be how the Egyptian state staffed its fields and state projects, and in the first millennium, we have cases of debt bondage to pay off debt. Private owners would often lease their fields to tenant farmers, who would be liable for a tax to their lessor. Temples largely functioned as independent economic units. Although they were subject to government control and some of their economies were intertwined with the state, temples could also be exempted from taxes and the compulsory labor imposed on them for state projects. Manufacturing industries and workshops, attached to government institutions and temples, processed raw materials (wood, stone, metals, textiles) and manufactured products— from pottery to architecture and ship-building.

Trade is well documented as early as Egyptian prehistory, both long-distance trade and local trade on marketplaces along the river, providing various outlets for the import and export of raw materials and finished goods. An important financial basis of Egypt's state economy was the gold mined in Nubia, and the value of all commodities produced and exchanged in Egypt was expressed in relation to a standard reference system—as a number of units of grain, copper, and silver (see also **Question 88**), thus anticipating the later invention of actual money in the first millennium BCE.

30.

Was climate change responsible for the end of the Old Kingdom?

Around 2200 BCE, Egypt's Old Kingdom came to an end, giving way to a period of regional power centers, the so-called First Intermediate Period. Egyptologists once thought they had a description of this collapse in the following passage from a literary text called *The Admonitions of Ipuwer*:

> Lo, the face is pale. ... Crime is everywhere. ... Lo, women are barren, none conceive. ... Lo, hearts are violent, storm sweeps the land, there's blood everywhere, no shortage of dead. ... Lo, many dead are buried in the river, the stream is the grave. ... Lo, the land turns like a potter's wheel. ... Lo, the river is blood, as one drinks from it one shrinks from people and thirsts for water. ... Towns are ravaged, Upper Egypt became wasteland. ... Lo, people are diminished. ... Lo, the desert claims the land, the nomes are destroyed, foreign bowmen have come into Egypt. ... There are no people anywhere. ... Lo, chests of ebony are smashed, precious *ssnḏm*-wood is chopped. ... Lo, tomb-builders have become field-laborers, those who were in the god's bark are yoked to it. ... Lo, merriment has ceased, is made no more, groaning is throughout the land, mingled with laments. ... No voice is straight in years of shouting, there is no end of shouting. ... Lo, children of nobles are smashed against walls, infants are put out on high ground. ... Lo, trees are felled, branches stripped. ... Gone is the gain of abundance of children.

> ... Lo, one eats herbs, washed down with water. ... Lo,
> the private chamber, its books are stolen. ... Lo, magic
> spells are divulged. ... Lo, the laws of the chamber are
> thrown out, men walk on them in the streets, beggars
> tear them up in the alleys. ... What the pyramid hid is
> empty. See now, the land is deprived of kingship. ... Men
> rebel against the Serpent [the Uraeus serpent as a symbol
> and protector of kingship].

Today, scholars are of the opinion that this is an ideological or
religious text, with no concrete reference to actual events. An
analogously skeptical judgment is also held for biographical
texts from this period, with their talk of famines and steps
taken to overcome crisis. These texts are generally viewed as
expressions of a literary motif glorifying a king or provincial
governor as a savior in times of need. Yet some texts—the
best-known example being that from the tomb of the governor
Ankhtify of Moalla—contain details too specific to be viewed
as purely literary. In particular, they speak of low Nile
inundations and irrigation measures. It has been scientifically
demonstrated that the climate became extremely dry in the
course of the third millennium; as early as Dynasties 1 and
2, the volume of the Nile had declined by around 30 percent.
Additionally, between 3000 and 2000 BCE, the level of the
Mediterranean sank by approximately five meters, while during
the second millennium there was scarcely any sedimentation of
the Nile (see **Question 13**). At the same time, we also observe
political changes: for instance, the provinces (with or without
the consent of the central government, we cannot be sure)
assumed more power, and eventually the central authority
lost all control over them. It is also possible that the Old
Kingdom state was distressed economically or incapable of
reacting to the new challenges. So far it has been impossible
to state conclusively which of these causal factors contributed
to the end of the Old Kingdom, whether such factors merely
accelerated an existing crisis of state, or whether the political
and economic problems are to be viewed as nothing more than
symptoms of the crisis. It is plausible, however, to think that a

combination of climatic, economic, and political developments brought the Old Kingdom to an end.

 # 31.

Why is the Middle Kingdom considered to be the "classical" period of ancient Egypt?

The Middle Kingdom (*c*.2000–1650 BCE) understood itself as a revival of the Old Kingdom; but its policies, and especially its literature and art, made it the classical epoch in the eyes of the following millennium of Egyptian history. After assuming power, the new rulers of Dynasty 12 implemented a comprehensive structural reform. South of the old capital city of Memphis, in the immediate vicinity of the royal pyramid complexes, Amenemhet I founded a new residence with the programmatic name *Itjtawy* "(Amenemhet,) who has taken possession of the Two Lands." The political succession was kept stable by the practice of early appointment of a coregent, thus preventing conflicts over succession to the throne. Political texts expounded the guidelines of the official understanding of the state and its civil service. Local provincial administrations ensured the efficient exploitation of resources, such as the alabaster quarries of Hatnub or—administered from Elephantine—the region of Nubia. It was the mid-Dynasty 12 King Senwosret III who eventually eliminated the system of hereditary provincial governorships in favor of a central administration. While the Old Kingdom had been concerned with the colonization of Lower Egypt, Senwosret II and Amenemhet III focused on the Faiyum, Egypt's largest oasis, which is connected to the Nile valley by a tributary. An extensive construction program lent this newly developed region a political and cultic character. The Middle Kingdom kings' construction policy was a central instrument in its internal and religious policy—for example, the promotion of Amun to the position of chief god of the kingdom and the dynasty, or the choice of the pyramid as the obligatory form of the royal tomb, aligning it with the Old Kingdom.

The economic power of the land was partially owed to extensive trade relations, which reached all the way to black Africa via the Sudan (Punt, Kerma), and via Byblos to Syria, as well as to the Aegean and Anatolia—as illustrated by the objects preserved in the "Tod treasure," the foundation deposit of the temple of Montu at Tod. There was also an unprecedented colonial policy, which enabled the exploitation of Nubia and the Sinai by turning them into Egyptian provinces. Within a period of 120 years (c.1930–1810 BCE), Egypt's southern boundary was extended into the Sudan south of the Second Cataract of the Nile, and the region was secured by a system of garrisoned fortresses and a provincial administration. In addition to the gold mines of Nubia, the raw materials of the Sinai (turquoise, copper), the galena mines on the Red Sea coast, and numerous stone quarries guaranteed the prosperity of the realm. The assumption that Egypt also cultivated an intensive foreign policy in the Levant, although so far scarcely documented, is nonetheless likely.

Along with an elite upper class, Egypt had a rather extensive middle class, and perhaps an even more differentiated society. The major cultural innovation of the Middle Kingdom was the production of extensive literature, including stories, didactic texts, and dialogues (such as the famous *Dialogue of a Man Weary of Life with His Soul*; see also **Question 74**). The Middle Kingdom thus became the classical period in the history of Egyptian literature, and the language of the period, Middle Egyptian, the classical form of the Egyptian language, remaining in use for historical and religious texts long after it ceased to be a living language, indeed, down into the Roman era (see also **Question 69**). Equally innovative and influential was the artistic production of the Middle Kingdom, as exemplified, for instance, in the superb royal portraiture of Dynasty 12.

32.

What role did the Hyksos play in Egypt's rise to a global power?

After the sudden collapse of Dynasty 13's sovereignty over all of Egypt around 1650 BCE, local rulers assumed power in various centers of the eastern Delta, some of whom called themselves "Hyksos" (Egyptian *ḥḳ3 ḫ3swt*, translated "rulers of foreign countries"). Although the Delta had a large Palestinian population, this was not a conquest of Egypt by foreign rulers, as scholars once thought, but an internal Egyptian phenomenon. The rulers of the most powerful of these dynasties, Dynasty 15, reigned from 1650 to 1530 BCE from their capital of Avaris (modern Tell el-Dab'a) in the eastern Delta. While their indirect Syro-Palestinian origin is clearly visible in their retention of cultural practices (grave goods, donkey and horse burials, religious architecture), they aligned themselves entirely with the Egyptian tradition in their royal ideology and many cultural policies. Influenced by texts from Dynasty 17, whose kings ultimately defeated the Hyksos, and by information handed down in texts of classical antiquity, scholars long perceived the Hyksos sovereignty as the historiographical template for all later instances of foreign rule over Egypt, continuing into modern times. Eduard Meyer, for instance, formulated the matter thus in his influential *History of Antiquity* (1884):

> At the turn from the 18th to the 17th c. BCE, the savage tribe of warriors to whose rulers Manetho gives the name 'Hyksos', burst into Egypt [...]. The foreign Barbarians wreaked havoc in Egypt, plundered the country and

destroyed the temples. They inflicted on the lands they ravaged the same devastation as later the Seljuks and Mongols, or earlier, in the middle of the 3rd millennium, the Gutians in Babylonia.

At the same time, Meyer and later scholars such as the pioneer of American Egyptology, James Henry Breasted, acknowledged the "incalculable debt" the ancient Egyptians owed to their conquerors by the fundamental transformations they spurred on the Nile: particularly the introduction of horse and chariot, and a new military ideology that facilitated the emergence of the Egyptian empire of the New Kingdom. The Hyksos Period thus appeared to be a decisive turning point in Egyptian history (see also **Question 28**).

Since then, scholars have become aware of the broader significance of cultural innovation in the history of the second millennium. Novelties and changes can be seen especially in the areas of military technology, fashion, religion, literature, and language. At first just a status symbol, the horse and chariot assumed military importance beginning in the fifteenth century BCE, when the maintenance of a chariot force led to the professionalization of the army, and newly available military career paths changed society profoundly. Numerous additional types of armor and weapons were introduced into Egypt at this time, such as the helmet, the coat of mail, daggers cast in one piece, the composite bow, a new form of battle axe, and the sickle sword; even Hittite shield moulds are attested. Demand for leatherwork, a Nubian specialty, was furthered by the introduction of new weapon technology from the Levant. Starting in the Hyksos Period, new textile production techniques and a new clothing style also made their way into Egypt: the vertical loom, new weaving techniques, new kinds of dyes for textiles and new types of ornamentation, and a multicolored clothing style at the royal court (see also **Question 98**). The excavators of the Delta residence of the later Ramesside kings at Qantir/Pi-Ramesses have uncovered integrated complexes of workshops. Here and in other places in Egypt, specialists also produced glassware, a favored luxury product of the elite.

Especially striking is the expansion of the Egyptian pantheon by deities of foreign origin (see **Question 50**). At the same time, during the second millennium, Egypt adopted literary themes and forms from western Asia, possibly leading to the development of a new type of narrative literature in Egypt.

It needs to be stressed, however, that when Egypt emerged as an imperial power, after 1500 BCE, allegedly stimulated by the Hyksos, territorial states also took shape all over the Ancient Near East: the kingdom of Mitanni, the Hittite, Middle Babylonian, Middle Assyrian, and Middle Elamite kingdoms, and the Mycenaean culture. It is thus plausible to suppose that even without Hyksos sovereignty, Egypt would have developed into a new territorial state, and that many of the innovations traced back to the Hyksos would in any case have found their way into Egypt.

 **33.**

How catastrophic was the Amarna Period for ancient Egypt?

The religious revolution of the Amarna Period—the reign of Amenhotep IV-Akhenaten (1353–1336 BCE)—has, abetted by various lucky accidents of preservation of evidence, met with a disproportionately large scholarly and public interest. Since the later nineteenth century, Akhenaten has been considered the first monotheist in world history, a harbinger of Christianity, or as a modernist who represented the triumph of reason and enlightened consciousness in history. At the same time, the expressionism of Amarna art has aroused considerable aesthetic interest, inspiring literature, music, and painting.

Characteristic of Akhenaten's religion was the increasingly exclusive worship of Aten, the sundisk itself, while the existence of other deities, at first still tolerated, was finally denied (Figure 7). The cult center of the religion was the newly founded sacred residence of Akhetaten (modern Amarna) in Middle Egypt, though the civil administration remained mostly in Memphis. The King himself changed his birth name *Amenhotep* ("Amun is content/provided") to *Akhenaten* ("he who is efficient for Aten"). After the major events of Akhenaten's twelfth regnal year, when the god Aten received a new titulary (an event previously dated to year 9) and Akhetaten was the stage for a great ceremonial presentation of tribute from foreign peoples, the sources dissipate (with the exception of the Amarna Letters, the foreign correspondence). Important individuals are no longer mentioned—perhaps they died (although Akhenaten's famous Queen Nefertiti, who was believed to have died by year 13, is now attested as late as year 16).

Akhenaten's theology declared Egypt's traditional religion to be in many respects false. It rejected the traditional mythical explanation of reality and founded its understanding on the first-hand observation of nature. In this religion, the light of the sun was the ultimate creative power and a proof of god's existence, while night and the netherworld were rejected as realms inimical to Aten. In the daily cult, Akhenaten assumed the function of a god on earth, especially the function of Amun, who was persecuted by Akhenaten. Art and architecture were committed to the new theology, which centered on the power of Aten and an idealized view of nature (see **Question 64**). Even the adoption of Late Egyptian, the spoken vernacular, as the official literary language should be seen as a consequence of the precise attention to reality demanded by Akhenaten.

Akhenaten's death was followed by a restoration of the old cults, as outlined in the Restoration Stela of Tutankhamun. Akhenaten's memory was eradicated; in official documents of Dynasty 19, he was called the "criminal of Amarna." In the same way that Akhenaten had eradicated the names and depictions of Amun in order to annihilate him, Akhenaten's names and depictions were now officially erased. Such a *damnatio memoriae* is well attested throughout Egyptian history for both kings and elite individuals; an earlier example is Queen Hatshepsut who proclaimed herself king in the early fifteenth century BCE and was erased from history by her successor, Thutmose III. Based on Akhenaten's persecution of the old religion and the subsequent reaction to the Amarna Period, some scholars have concluded that Amarna was one of Egypt's most traumatic episodes, one that lingered long in the cultural memory, even into texts of the Graeco-Roman era.

Against this view is the fact that Akhenaten implemented his religion only to a very limited degree. On the boundary stelae of Amarna, Akhenaten himself vowed not to spread the new ideology beyond the area of the city itself. Outside the capital, the old religion seems to have continued as before, and even in Amarna, the population seems to have continued to worship deities other than Aten. It is uncertain whether opponents of the regime were persecuted, as surmised by some scholars. The persecution of traditional deities was not a general iconoclasm, but rather directed specifically against Amun and his consort Mut. Thus the period should not be viewed as having caused a general trauma.

We would probably be able to understand the demise of and response to Amarna if we knew why this unique period of Egyptian history came about in the first place. Traditionally, scholars have assumed that Akhenaten's revolution was directed at the growing political and economic influence of the priesthood of Amun. From this point of view, the new religion was politically motivated, with Akhenaten as the protagonist of a group concerned with the decline in royal power. In fact, Akhenaten assumed one of the functions previously ascribed to Amun—as supporter and helper of the faithful. According to a second scenario, the impetus to the revolution was intellectual—Akhenaten's theology of Aten was supposedly a reaction to a cognitive crisis. This theory sees Akhenaten alone as the driving force behind Amarna, the promulgator of a new truth. The most recent explanation, however, ascribes the Amarna Period to external factors. Only an unprecedented event could have discredited Amun and inspired support for Akhenaten's implementation of Atenism, with all its theological, social, and economic consequences. Such an event could have been the plague that devastated the ancient Near East in the second half of the fourteenth century BCE. The plague would explain why Amenhotep III, Akhenaten's father, dedicated 730 statues to the goddess Sakhmet-Mut, Amun's consort and goddess of plague, and why the Syrian storm-god Baal, a redeemer from plague, was elevated into a new state god of Egypt immediately after the end of Amarna (see also **Question 50**). To overcome the plague, the elite of the state might have decided, as a last resort, to give Akhenaten a free hand in introducing a new religion. The King's failure would thus have sealed the fate of his religion, and his own fate as well. In this scenario, any traumatic effect of the Amarna Period would be due not to Akhenaten's changes but to the plague, which would have affected wide segments of the population.

 **34.**

Why were love poems only written in the Ramesside Period?

All Egyptian love poems known thus far range in date from early Dynasty 19 to the middle of Dynasty 20—that is, for most of the epoch we call the Ramesside Period. There are other text genres, such as the Harper's Songs, that are also written in Late Egyptian and attested only from this period. In particular, we may point to texts with burlesque or satirical content, and to the magnificent tales of the Ramesside Period: the Tale of the Two Brothers, the Contendings of Horus and Seth, the Tale of Apophis and Seqenenre, the Tale of the Taking of Joppa, the Tale of Isis and Re, the Tale of the Doomed Prince, and the Tale of Khonsemhab and the Ghost. Also from this period, but documented only on illustrated papyri or in the form of individual representations, we have animal fables and other tales that often represent a topsy-turvy world (see **Question 91**). There are also innovations in monumental inscriptions— as in the account of the Battle of Qadesh under Ramesses II, in autobiographies, and in certain other text genres—as well as in the visual arts. It seems clear that there must already have been (oral) precursors of these love poems, Harper's Songs, and other genres in Dynasty 18, and that changed conventions led to their being fixed in writing and more widely circulated only at this time.

Interestingly, at the beginning of the Ramesside Period (*c.*1300 BCE), Sety I proclaimed an era called "Renaissance" (as Ramesses XI would do again over two centuries later, at the end of this period). It was the Amarna Period which, by making Late Egyptian the official written language, stimulated this cultural innovation, a sort of modernism. But the Ramesside Period had an innovative character in other respects as well. In documentation from all strata of society we find displays of a new central motif: "personal piety," an explicit turning to the gods, whose authority and decisive power now penetrated all areas of private and official life. A prime example is supplied by the report of the Battle of Qadesh, in which Ramesses II turns to Amun for help and then credits the god with averting an impending defeat. The Instruction of Amenemope counsels submission to divine will, and oracles were increasingly consulted in political decision making and in other areas of life.

35.

How un-Egyptian was the Libyan Period?

Beginning in Dynasty 20, Libyans, who constituted a large part of the Egyptian military, acquired ever more political influence; and when the New Kingdom came to an end, they assumed power over Egypt for the next 350 years (Figure 8). From Dynasty 21 on, which was presumably already of Libyan origin, there were two power centers: the new capital city of Tanis in the Delta, which replaced Pi-Ramesses as the Residence of the royal house, and which was also the burial place of the Egyptian kings; and Thebes, the center of a "theocracy of Amun" under the regency of the high priest of Amun. The Theban royal tombs were now emptied at the initiative of the state, which treated the tomb treasures as a short-term substitute for the loss of Egypt's foreign possessions and their revenues. Such a turn of events is conceivable only against the background of a new religious ideology that viewed Amun as the true king of Egypt and the kings as mere priests.

The Libyan Period presents the picture of a territory split up into several individual states. In the middle of the eighth century, the Delta alone consisted of as many as a dozen different principalities, the largest of which was the west Delta realm of the rulers of Sais. Among the questions most hotly debated by scholars are whether or not a series of political and cultural phenomena in this era can be ultimately traced back to the Libyans themselves, and whether or not the Libyan Period can be considered a period of foreign rule. In the later first millennium, the Persians and the Greeks counted as foreign rulers, while the Kushites of Dynasty 25, whose origin lay in the Sudan, did not. In their official documents, the Libyans were devoted to Egyptian religion and used the Egyptian language and writing system, but this says nothing about their cultural identity (or their actual mastery of Egyptian!). Quite to the contrary, they retained signs of their foreign origin: their leaders were designated "chieftains of the Libyans," they bore Libyan names, and they had themselves depicted wearing the Libyan feather on their heads even in their exercise of Egyptian offices, including priestly offices. On the other hand, it must be said that it was now possible to depict foreign cultural origin more freely than had been the case, for instance, in the time of the Hyksos. The very splintering of Egypt into states that relied on a warrior class who pledged fealty to the ruler and were rewarded with fiefs has been viewed as a Libyan cultural feature. But it can also be understood as a symptom of the crisis that saw the collapse of territorial states throughout the eastern Mediterranean world at this time (see also **Question 24**).

Other cultural changes can similarly be explained by changes in basic conditions rather than as being due to specifically Libyan influence; for example, the end of the custom of private tombs, which in Dynasty 21 led to a rich religious iconography on coffins. It is also true, however, that the Libyan Period entailed a brave new direction for Egypt. The building activity undertaken at Tanis by the Libyan kings transformed the city into a "new Thebes." Along with a new Luxor-style temple, temples for Amun, Khonsu, and Mut were erected in Tanis, creating the equivalent of the temple of Karnak in Upper Egyptian Thebes; even their names corresponded to those of the Theban temples. Similarly, the Tanite royal tombs discovered in 1939 by Pierre Montet also followed (with the exception of the very first tombs) Theban New Kingdom tradition in their decoration and furnishings, though their location in the temple court and the inclusion of family members and officials in the royal tomb were innovations. The analogy to the Valley of the Kings was completed under Shoshenq III, when the entire Tanite royal necropolis was vaulted over by a huge mountain of bricks, thereby creating an artificial equivalent to Thebes where the tombs had been hewn into the mountain rock.

Figure 8: Small figurine made of bronze with gold and black gold inlay, depicting a Libyan—with bands crossed over the chest, long hair, short beard. In the Libyan period from which this figure dates (*c*.800 BCE), Libyan military rulers reigned in Lower Egypt

This architectural emulation of the sacred city of Thebes made Lower Egypt culturally independent of the southern half of the land, and Upper Egypt was now and for all times reduced to the status of a province. From this point forward, all of Egypt's metropolises would lie in or on the edge of the hub that the Delta represented in terms of trade, communication, and the need for spatial expansion. Tanis thus signified a decision to concentrate Egyptian traditions in a new locale that was capable of survival. If this decision was made by Libyans, Egypt owes to them a new framework in which it could survive.

# 36.

Did private individuals make the history of Egypt's Late Period?

From the point of view of nineteenth-century historicism, history was above all political history, created by historical personalities. Twentieth-century historians emphasized the importance of currents of history other than individuals— social and economic developments, climate and mentality, and so forth. Nonetheless, it remains uncontested that momentous individuals contribute to changes in history, sometimes vital ones. The ancient Egyptian tradition stressed the central role of kingship, though for the most part we cannot discern to what extent individual throneholders or the "men behind the king" (Wolfgang Helck) made the political decisions. It is significant, however, that starting in the Early Dynastic Period (at first in tomb architecture and tomb sculpture), individuals—first princes, later individuals unrelated to the royal family—emerge who claim their share in the shaping of Egyptian politics. Autobiographies first appeared during the transition to Dynasty 4, centuries before statements about the individual person of the king were recorded. These texts stress the achievements of officials in their capacity as expedition leaders, construction supervisors, or administrators. In the second millennium, high state officials, army generals, and high priests unquestionably had significant means, influence, and political power. In the first millennium, this development led to an even more pluralistic political situation.

Texts from the transition to the first millennium clearly demonstrate the weakness of kingship at that time. In one

literary text, the envoy Wenamun is portrayed as being robbed
and humiliated in the Levant, whereas Amun is the actual lord
of the world (the protagonist's name means "Amun exists").
According to another text, a supposed priest of Heliopolis was
discharged from office and banished, while the addressee of
his letter led a good life "in the keeping of the sun god." A
Demotic story, the tale of the court official Merib and Pharaoh
Badja, relates an incredible sequence of events. King Badja is
kidnapped by his conniving court chancellor and abandoned,
utterly helpless, in the mountains of Syria. Merib succeeds in
rescuing him and restoring justice to the land of Egypt. Though
this episode is assuredly fictive, it symbolizes the considerable
scope of action possible for non-royal individuals during the
Late Period. Offices were now inherited over the course of many
generations, and the subsequent political and economic rise of
families—we have documentation, for example, of the veritable
family saga of Petiese—resulted in an increasing independence
of high officials from the kingship. They could even describe
the king as dependent on them, as in the following inscription
of the dignitary Hor:

> He (the king!) lived on hearing my tongue (speak). I
> led the king to the wellbeing of the two banks, (for) I
> sailed on the water of the god [= I was a loyal follower
> of the god]. He founded the Two Lands according to the
> conceptions of my heart (!), and I set out to maintain the
> banks in life.

The highest state officials of Dynasties 25 and 26, some of
whom had themselves buried in gigantic palatial tombs at
Thebes, were thoroughly candid about the leading role they
played in history. Prominent examples include Montuemhet,
mayor of Thebes during the Assyrian occupation of Egypt (and
thus called "king of Thebes" in the Assyrian documents!), and
Udjahorresnet, an influential general and priest at the time of
the Persian invasion of Egypt.

37.

Were the ancient Egyptians awaiting a Messiah?

A series of texts preserved in Egyptian (Demotic) or in Greek translation, all of them from the Graeco-Roman Period, prophesy the coming of a savior-king and the reestablishment of an era of wellbeing. We may thus call them messianic texts, though their interpretation and even their chronological order have been the object of considerable controversy. The best-known is the so-called Demotic Chronicle, which dates to the early Ptolemaic Period—that is, the third century BCE. In essence, it contains oracular pronouncements that are explained in light of the history of the last native dynasties, the Second Persian Occupation of the fourth century, and the early Ptolemaic Period. Almost without exception, the last native kings of Egypt are judged negatively, while the rule of the Greeks is viewed in a positive light and prophesied a long duration. The prophecy of a future savior-king who will rule in Herakleopolis can thus in no way be understood as a voice of nationalistic Egyptian opposition. In contrast, the second-century BCE text known as the Potter's Oracle displays a decidedly anti-Greek and anti-government character. After a period of disaster, the city of the "belt-wearers"—Alexandria—will be abandoned, and under a savior-king there will be a period in which the Nile will once more flow abundantly, winter and summer will occur at the correct times of the year, and the winds will again blow from the right direction. Yet another text, the Lamb of Bocchoris, is preserved in a copy from the year 4 CE. It relates a fictive prophecy from the sixth and last year of King Bocchoris

(720 BCE) which foretells a disastrous period of 900 years' duration, followed by a period of wellbeing under a savior-king, evidently at the end of Egypt's many successive foreign rulerships.

These and other texts stand in the tradition of earlier Egyptian literary works in which history is conceived of as the fulfillment of a prophecy (see also **Questions 75** and **76**). An example is the Prophecy of Neferti, in which a ruler "Ameny" (maybe Amenemhet I, the founder of Dynasty 12) is represented as a savior-king who brings an end to a period of disaster and injustice. This contrast is also a constant ideological motif that was widely used in royal texts from the beginning of a reign, attested examples including texts of Tutankhamun, Haremhab, and Ramesses IV. In these texts the period before the beginning of the reign is portrayed as a time of crisis, which is overcome all the more splendidly (also foretold by miraculous omens) with the new ruler's assumption of power. A symbol of the demise of ancient Egypt is found in the last of these descriptions of disaster, the Apocalypse of Asclepius from the fourth century CE, which no longer cherishes any hopes of salvation by a god or a royal messiah:

> This land, once the seat of religion, will then be bereft of divine presence. Foreigners will inhabit this land, and not only will the old cults be neglected, but religion, piety, and the cult of the gods will be actively prohibited by law. Of the Egyptian religion only fables will remain and inscribed stones [...]. The gods will turn away from men—o painful separation!—and only the evil demons will remain, mingling with men and driving their wretched victims by force into all kinds of crime—into war, robbery, fraud, and everything hateful to the nature of the soul. Then will the earth no longer be solid and the sea no longer navigable, the heavens will not hold the stars in their orbits, nor will the stars keep to their course in the firmament. Every divine voice will necessarily fall silent. The fruits of the earth will rot, the soil will become barren, the very air will be

oppressive and heavy. And these things will hold sway
in the senescent world: absence of religion, of order,
and of solidarity.

Perhaps not incorrectly, Christian authors such as Lactantius
and Augustine saw this text as expressing Egypt's acknowledgment of its own demise, conveyed at a time when the
guarantees of Egyptian world order—kingship and temple
cult—could no longer be taken for granted.

4

Egyptian Religion

38.

Can we understand ancient Egyptian religion?

Can academic scholarship, oriented as it is to first-hand proof, understand Egyptian religion? What were the criteria of reality and rationality in ancient Egypt? According to what model can we understand what seems irrational to us? Is it not the case that our traditional distinctions—rational vs. mystical, profane vs. sacred, natural vs. supernatural—are modern concepts that are scarcely helpful, and perhaps even counterproductive, in explaining Egyptian religion? A glance at scholarship on Egyptian religion since the nineteenth century reveals its biases towards contemporaneous concepts. Around 1900, evolutionary views of religion prevailed, seeing religion as a stage in the development from magic to science. Within religion itself, scholars believed in a progressive development from animism to monotheism. In 1934, Adolph Erman pronounced Egyptian religion to be an "abstruse polytheism" for which "we modern profane people clearly lack the correct understanding." For ancient Egypt, he observed a continuous religious development whose climax would have been reached with the monotheism of the Amarna Period and a personal relationship of faith between man and the divine. In the same year, his American former student and colleague James Henry Breasted laid even more stress on this evolutionary notion. It was in the religion of the Ramesside Period that he recognized "the profoundest expression of the devotional religious spirit ever attained by the men of Egypt"; namely, the birth of conscience. This led Breasted to view Egyptian religious development as the precursor of biblical religion and

European morality. In 1941, Hermann Kees projected ancient Egypt's cultural decay, which he believed he saw occurring from the New Kingdom on, onto religion as well; in his view, the Old Kingdom was the original and genuine period in which Egyptian religion blossomed.

In the post-World War II era scholars realized that such modern value judgments could not lead to an understanding of Egyptian religion. They thus turned away from historical treatments of Egyptian religion, devoting themselves instead to the study of religious phenomena and structures. In the *History of Religious Ideas*, the religious scholar Mircea Eliade had, in a programmatic manner, pointed to the existence of religious constants: "The 'sacred' is an element in the structure of consciousness, and not a mere stage in the development of that consciousness." But when Henri Frankfort emphasized in 1948, in support of this new focus on religious constants, that the ancient Egyptians believed they lived in a static, unchanging world, so that it is "neither possible nor necessary" to write a history of Egyptian religion, this was yet another modern misperception. Out of all the areas of Egyptian culture, it is Egyptian religion where clear-cut changes over time are most visible. Even so, Frankfort was the first to criticize the Eurocentric view of Egyptian religion, noting that it is often impossible to translate Egyptian concepts into our own cultural language. In Frankfort's opinion, Greek logic stood in contrast to the Egyptian principle of a "multiplicity of approaches," according to which certain questions can receive several responses that are not mutually exclusive. Thus, for example, accounts of creation juxtapose different ideas. According to the doctrine of Hermopolis, the sun god emerged from a lotus blossom that rose out of the primeval ocean, but we are also told that he emerged from an egg on the primeval mound that had risen out of the primeval ocean. In the 1940s and 1950s, attempts to systematize basic phenomena of Egyptian religion touched on such issues as the multiplicity of divine forms of manifestation, and the "composite gods" whose very names indicate the association of two or more deities, such as Amun-Re, Ptah-Sokar-Osiris, or Harmakhis-Khepri-Re-Atum. Hans

Bonnet saw this phenomenon as a specific characteristic of Egyptian religion, for which he coined the concept of syncretism (1952). According to Bonnet, in Dynasty 19 Egyptian religion arrived at a pantheism in which the highest god dwelled in all the others, though the traditional polytheistic beliefs stood in the way of this tendency towards an ideal monotheism.

The most comprehensive study from the point of view of the phenomenology of religion (describing religion through the experience of its worshippers) came from the pen of the theologian Siegfried Morenz (*Egyptian Religion*, 1960). Morenz considered the faith of the ancient Egyptians to be the most important phenomenon, and, in his judgment, genuine understanding was possible only under the assumption "that one has to have experienced oneself the meaning of religion and of God if one is to interpret from the sources the relationship between God and man in an age remote from our own." Nevertheless, in his slightly later work, *The Rise of the Transcendent God in Egypt* (1964), Morenz traced a line of historical development that (in the opinion of Morenz and others) culminated in the universal god of the Ramesside Period. Yet at the same time, Eberhard Otto stressed even more emphatically than others the central antagonism between the idea of a solar sky god (Amun-Re) and a god of the dead (Osiris). In his groundbreaking work *The One and The Many* (1971), Erik Hornung identified the question of the unity and multiplicity of divine concepts as the fundamental problem in the study of Egyptian religion. According to him, the affirmation of Morenz and others that there was a monotheism hidden behind the multiplicity of deities was, to be sure, "a grandiose, western-style perspective—but it has little in common with Egyptian ways of looking and thinking." Decisive, in Hornung's view, is Egyptian ontology, in which the differentiated and changing world to which the gods belong stands opposed to an undifferentiated world that existed before creation and continues to exist beyond it. Hornung also stressed the complementary logic of the ancient Egyptians, which he opposed to classical two-valued logic (where the only possible truth values for the meaning behind a declaration are either true or false), a point of view that has again found its critics.

During the second half of the twentieth century, as it became clearer how much Egyptian religion had changed in the course of its history, the use of phenomenological and systematic approaches began to be questioned. There was a veritable renaissance in historical studies devoted to assessments of specific eras. In this respect, Jan Assmann has proved to be one of the most influential scholars of Egyptian religion in the last three decades, through such studies as *The Search for God in Ancient Egypt* (1984) and *The Mind of Egypt* (1995). In Assmann's work, we again see an attempt to trace a historical development, one whose high point he identifies—like Bonnet—as the pantheistic-transcendent cosmic god of the Ramesside Period. Contemporary discussion has included a caution against overly selective and simplistic conclusions, while John Baines and others have advocated the study of religion as a social, institutional, and economic phenomenon. In particular, a history of Egyptian religion must take into account the relationship between religion and kingship ("temple and palace"), whose changing significance is apparent in architecture: from the Old Kingdom, we have no divine temples or temples that were marginal at best; the New Kingdom produced huge temples to the gods as well as huge funerary temples to the kings; and in the Late Period, the temples of the gods were huge, while royal funerary temples were nonexistent or marginal.

 **39.**

What was ancient Egypt's most important religious concept?

Maat, a term whose meaning encompasses "correctness," "orderedness," and "balance," is generally viewed as the basic concept of the Egyptian world view. Modern translations like "truth," "justice," "right," or "cosmic order" capture only individual aspects of the concept. The idea of *Maat* also includes solidarity, lawfulness, and accountability in human society, essentially the right structure of life, which enables *Maat* to continue. Half a century ago, Rudolf Anthes offered this formulation:

> Maat holds this little world together and makes it a part of the cosmic order. It is the delivery of grain; it is the uprightness of human beings in thought, word, and deed; it is the faithful conduct of the administration; it is the king's prayers and offerings to the divine; it permeates the economy, the administration, the cult, the law.

According to a statement in the royal morning ritual, the sun god instituted the Egyptian king on earth to put *Maat* into effect and abolish its opposite, *isfet* (often understood, or translated, as chaos). At the same time, the king was answerable to *Maat*; that is, he did not stand above order, he was a part of it (see **Question 46**). Gods, kings, and men also lived on *Maat*; thus, in an important cult act, the king offered the gods a figurine depicting *Maat*, here personified as a goddess. The so-called "*Maat* litany" of the New Kingdom contains the following formula concerning the sun god: "O Re, *lord* of *Maat*, who *lives* on *Maat*," and an inscription of Hatshepsut states, "I have magnified *Maat*, which he (Re) loves, for I have understood that he lives on it. It is (also) my nourishment, I swallow its dew, being of one substance with him."

A functioning network of social relationships was essential to the preservation of *Maat* in society. An ethically correct life was demanded, and forbidden were egoism, enrichment at the expense of others, or injury to others by force or through falsehoods. The *Complaints of the Eloquent Peasant* (*c*.2000 BCE) declares:

> He who lessens falsehood fosters Maat,
> He who fosters the good reduces evil,
> As satiety's coming removes hunger,
> Clothing removes nakedness;
> As the sky is serene after a storm,
> Warming all who shiver;
> As fire cooks what is raw,
> As water quenches thirst.

The individual affirmed that he unceasingly fulfilled *Maat*, as in the autobiography of Padisobek: "I rejoiced over words of *Maat*, my abomination was hearing lies. I did *Maat* on earth as many times as there are hairs on a head." Existence in the afterlife was in large part dependent on society, which assured the provisioning of the deceased through the funerary cult and its offerings, but only righteous conduct during life guaranteed the transfer of the deceased's possessions after death. Ethical conduct was also the precondition for a successful outcome at the Judgment of the Dead in the "Hall of Perfect *Maat*," an ordeal for which the deceased also equipped themselves with plenty of magical aids, such as the Book of the Dead papyrus or amulets (see also **Question 51**). In the so-called "negative confession" of the Book of the Dead (spell 125), the deceased recites a lengthy litany, assuring the forty-two judges of the dead that he or she had not offended against *Maat*:

I have not done crimes against people; I have not mistreated cattle [...]. I have not done any harm. [...] I have not blasphemed a god. I have not robbed the poor. I have not done what the god abhors. I have not maligned a servant to his master. I have not caused pain. I have not caused tears. I have not killed. I have not ordered to kill. I have not made anyone suffer. I have not damaged the offerings in the temples [...]. I have not (wrongly) copulated nor defiled myself. I have not increased nor reduced the measure [...]. I have not cheated in the fields. I have not added to the weight of the balance, I have not falsified the plummet of the scales. I have not taken milk from the mouth of children. I have not deprived cattle of their pasture. I have not snared birds in the reeds of the gods, I have not caught fish in their ponds. I have not held back water in its season [...]. I have not quenched a needed fire. I have not neglected the days of meat offerings [...]. I have not stopped a god in his procession. I am pure! I am pure! I am pure! I am pure!

These statements amount to an authoritative codification of *Maat*. At the weighing of the heart, the heart, as embodiment of the deceased's conduct during life, was placed on one pan of a scale, and it was not supposed to outweigh *Maat*, who could be depicted either as a feather or as a goddess figurine, that was on the other pan. In order not to run any risk, the representations of the scene in the Book of the Dead papyri depict a positive outcome—the pan with the heart is the lighter one—and thus magically anticipate the desired result (see **Question 40**).

Figure 9: Hypocephalus of a woman Tasheritkhons—a disk placed under the head of the deceased, with the depiction of a variety of deities (the four-headed creator god in the middle; the goddess Hathor; the serpent Nehebkau; the god Min) and an inscription that provided protection to the head by heat or a flame

 **40.**

How did Egyptian magic function?

"Magic" and "sorcery" are biased terms from western culture. Since they often evoke (false) negative associations, they should be used only with great care in describing Egyptian practices. Nineteenth- and twentieth-century Egyptologists viewed magic as an archaic stage of cultural development, a product of the allegedly infantile and ignorant thinking of early humankind. In 1899, the widely read British Egyptologist E.A.W. Budge wrote in his book on *Egyptian Magic*:

> When we consider the lofty spiritual character of the greater part of the Egyptian religion, and remember its great antiquity, it is hard to understand why the Egyptians carefully preserved in their writings and ceremonies so much which savoured of gross and childish superstition, and which must have been the product of their predynastic or prehistoric ancestors, even during the period of their greatest intellectual enlightenment.

His contemporary Adolf Erman wrote in the same vein in his *Egyptian Religion* of 1934:

> Magic is a barbarous offshoot of religion [...] When once the ideas of a nation have struck out in this direction—and it is precisely the youthful unsophisticated nations that are most readily attracted by it—there is no check on it, and by the side of the noble plant of religion there

flourishes this fantastic weed of magic. With nations
of limited understanding it completely stifles religion
and there ensues a barbarism, where the magical fetish
is the supreme object, and where the sorcerer with his
hocus-pocus takes the place of the priest. No one would
wish to ascribe a similar condition of affairs to such a
youthful nation as the ancient Egyptians; it would be as
incongruous as it would be to compare the imbecility of
a childish old man with the folly of a promising youth.
But the Egyptian people shared very fully, and also at an
early period, in this absurdity.

Today, however, scholars understand that what Egyptian
texts call *heka* ("magic") was a comprehensive, nearly techno-
scientific, and precisely thought-out and rigorous system that
was realized through texts, objects, and actions. Ancient
Egyptian magic, which was present as an underlying structure
of the cosmos even at the time of creation, stabilized or restored
the existing order of the world. It was employed in all spheres
of Egyptian life—to ward off diseases, to assure life in the
hereafter, to sustain the cosmos, to protect against attacks
from outside and rebellion from within, and to safeguard home
and fields (Figure 9). As the Instruction for Merikare states in
reference to the creator god's deeds on behalf of humankind,
"He made for them magic as weapons to ward off the blow of
events, guarding them by day and by night." Magic thus played
an auxiliary role in many aspects of ancient Egyptian culture,
including medicine, temple cult, military and diplomatic
activities, ethics, and education. Its function as protection and
weapon is vividly represented in two scenes from the Book of
Gates. The gods hold up throw-nets out of which magic is cast
upon Apopis, the serpent of chaos, who threatens the continued
existence of the cosmos.

In ancient Egypt the practice of magic followed set rules
and requirements to insure that the world functioned properly.
Threatened or chaotic elements of the cosmos were restored
and integrated into the established order by analogizing or
identifying them with an element of the structured world.

Thus, for instance, the patient was equated with the sick Horus-child who, by way of mythic precedent, was cured by his mother Isis. Since the patient was ritually equated with him, the patient would inevitably become healthy. Similar analogies could generally be made regarding the individual in question, the magician, magical objects (like amulets; see **Question 51**), or magical language. In each case, restoration of order was inevitable, for otherwise, the element (Horus, Osiris, the sun god, the cosmos) associated with the problem in question would perish. It was not until the Late Period—that is, the second half of the first millennium BCE—that magic intended to gain power or do harm—a kind of magic basically foreign to the original system—made its appearance in Egypt. Christianity stigmatized Egyptian magic, as well as Roman magical practices, as fraud, witchery, and occultism; it was only at this time that magic in Egypt came to be viewed as something contrary to religious and social norms.

41.

What does the phrase "grammar of the temple" mean?

From the Egyptian point of view (see **Question 37** and the Apocalypse of Asclepius cited there), the functions of a temple had to be properly maintained in order to preserve the cosmos, for on the ritual level, the temple was an image of the cosmos. The deities who inhabited the cosmos dwelled in their statues to receive offerings and adoration, and to make their will known to humankind (see also **Question 42**). The equation of temple and cosmos functioned via correlations that were clearly marked out in the temple's thematic, artistic, and architectural layout. The path from the entrance to the innermost sanctuary inclined gently upward, with the result that the holy of holies, on its flat platform or terrace, was situated in an elevated place. This terrace represented the first piece of land (the primeval mound) that emerged from the water of the primeval ocean at the beginning of the world. The deity, as the creator and guarantor of the cosmos, sat in its shrine inside the holy of holies. The first land to emerge from the primeval ocean consisted of black earth, hence the floors of the Old Kingdom pyramid temples were made of black basalt. On the temple walls, the lowest register of the decoration was either painted black or it depicted papyrus thickets growing out of the earth, and often also so-called "fecundity figures." The holy of holies was hidden behind a grove of papyrus plants, lotus blossoms, or palm trees, which were rendered in the form of stone columns that rose up into the sky and represented the vegetation that grew on the primeval mound. Each temple roof was the sky itself, which (in some cases preserved to this day) was painted blue and decorated with stars, and many temples, such as that at Dendara, also had astronomical ceilings. Falcons and vultures flying in the sky as well as winged sundisks were depicted above the central passageways through these temples. And in the temple courtyard, well shafts led down to the ground water, which was believed to rise up from the primeval ocean that still surrounded the earth. These symbolic references to the cosmos were complemented by more tangible ones that can be seen in the construction of the temple itself. The cosmos was gathered together in the temple in the form of stone from the eastern and western deserts, the precious metals that were used, the materials set into the carved decoration, the booty from military expeditions that was stored in the temple treasury, and—as in the "Botanical Garden" of Thutmose III at Karnak (see **Question 18**)—the representations of exotic animals and plants. Also worth noting is the way the walls surrounding the temple compound were constructed: the courses of brick were laid in the form of huge waves that suggested the primeval ocean encircling the world. Historical descriptions of high Nile inundations that flooded the temples directly compare the temples rising out of the water with the world immediately after creation.

The meaningfulness of the world finds expression in the fact that the arrangement of all texts and decoration on the temple walls are coordinated with one another. Thus, for instance, certain deities correspond to one another at equivalent places in the temple, creating a highly complex system of relationships and meaning that we are only beginning to recognize and understand. We call this system the "grammar of the temple" (an expression coined by Philippe Derchain), and the ancient Egyptians believed it stemmed from divine inspiration, as indicated in a text from the temple of Edfu which relates that it was built "as it had been begun by the ancestors, and as it is written in the great plan of that book which fell from the sky north of Memphis." The temple's decoration corresponded to the cosmological organization of the world: the north side equaling Lower Egypt, the south Upper Egypt, the east the rising sun, and the west the setting sun. The gateway or pylon of the temple (which emulated the shape of two hills) was understood to be the mountains supporting the sky in the western and eastern desert, the place where the sun set and rose, while the central axis through the length of the temple reflected the course of the sun through the sky. The interior walls of the temple represented the interior of the ordered world—that is, Egypt—and their decoration was concerned mostly with the temple cult and the relationship between the king and the gods and goddesses. The outer walls, though, were devoted mostly to the chaotic world outside Egypt; it is here that we often find representations of battles and hunting scenes. The rainspouts attached to the outer walls could be in the form of lions, which were directed against Egypt's external enemies. Certain texts combine the cosmic symbolism of the temple with the actual geography of the world—for instance, when the (in reality very small) Sacred Lake next to the temple of Abydos is ritually identified with the Mediterranean Sea, whose size no one knew and on whose banks the cedars of Lebanon grew:

> The lake before it is like the sea, whose extent no one can see, clear like the color of lapis lazuli. In its midst grows a daily abundance of papyrus, reeds, and lotus blossoms; a flock of birds lands in it to take pleasure. Around it grow trees that reach up to the sky, thriving like the cedars on the Lebanon.

Even the temporal structure of the world is transplanted into certain temples. At Edfu, the decoration of the columns behind the gateway displays the festivals of the calendar. As the shadows of the gateway moved along in the course of the year, they revealed the sections with those festivals that occurred during that very part of the year.

42.

Why did the high priest wipe away his footprints as he exited the temple?

Egyptian religion was a religion of secrecy (see **Question** 52). The rituals celebrated in the temple, which were also called "secrets," were not allowed to be generally known, so that their effectiveness would not be compromised, and their performance was restricted to only a small circle of priests. A ritual text for maintaining the world, in which a figure of Osiris representing the life of Egypt was replaced by a new one at the beginning of the new year, states explicitly: "It must remain very, very secret, unknown and unseen. No one but the sundisk can look into its mystery." In an Egyptian temple, the holy of holies was a closed-off room containing the cult image of the deity, which was hidden in a shrine. It was approached through various antechambers, and on its three remaining sides, it was shielded from the world outside by several walls; only the high priest of the deity had access to it. The daily ritual of the god or goddess began in the morning with a hymn sung by the priests to waken the deity, after which his or her body (*i.e.*, statue) was anointed, newly clothed, and presented with offerings. After the completion of the ritual, which was also performed in briefer versions at midday and in the evening, the high priest closed and sealed the door of the shrine and then left the sanctuary, always facing the shrine and the door of the holy of holies, sweeping away the footprints he had left in the sand or on the sand-covered stone floor. Thus he erased the traces of his proximity to the deity, of his penetration into the sacred space, of his beholding the divine mystery. Even on the occasion of processions in which the divine image was carried out of the temple for such purposes as visiting other sanctuaries, it remained covered. Special collections of magical spells, the books "Protection of the House" and "Protection of the Body," shielded the temple and the cult image, which was understood as a living body, from danger.

The protection of this mystery ended with Christianity. In the fourth and fifth centuries CE, the spiritual leaders of the Egyptian Christians recorded the destruction of Egyptian temples: the cult statues were removed from the holy of holies and then smashed or burned, and representations on the temple walls were chiseled away. Other temples had already been profaned in the Roman era, as happened to the temple of Luxor, which was converted into a Roman military camp in 301 CE. The violation of Egyptian temples was effected in three ways: unauthorized and impure persons entered the most sacred parts of the temples, cultic equipment was destroyed, and the temple cult and rituals were discontinued.

43.

What did the ancient Egyptians dream and how were dreams interpreted?

The usual Egyptian word for "dream" is derived from a verb meaning "(a)waken." Dreams thus probably indicated a sort of waking state, or, at least a conscious, alert perception during sleep. According to the so-called "Calendars of Lucky and Unlucky Days" (hemerologies), which list the "good" and "bad" days of a year according to certain omens and were probably used in temples, dreams provided information regarding events to come. Actual dream books are preserved to us from the New Kingdom (one book only) and in the form of Demotic texts from the Roman Period in Egypt. The Ramesside dream book (Papyrus Chester Beatty III) that once belonged to a scribe named Qenherkhopshef from Deir el-Medina, the settlement that was home to the workmen who prepared the royal tombs on the west bank of Thebes, contains 227 dreams and their interpretations. Two thirds of these are good omens and one third bad ones. The dreams are arranged according to specific types of instances, as is also the case in medical and legal handbooks: "If someone sees himself in a dream drowning in the river: good, (it means) purification from all evil." The explanation of the dreams made use of their images and symbolism, or of puns based on the association of similar words, which, as the Egyptians understood it, created a meaningful connection between the two elements (see also **Question 79**). For example, "If someone sees himself in a dream bringing mice from the field: bad, (it means) a bitter heart"—in this case, the words for "mouse" and "bitter" sounded similar in ancient Egyptian. In a dream, contact could also be made between a person and a deity. Deities appeared to royalty, either to lend support for their political activity or to incite them to specific deeds, and occasionally, to private persons as well. According to his Giza stela inscription, as crown prince Thutmose (IV) slept at the foot of the Great Sphinx of Giza and dreamt that the god Harmakhis, whom the sphinx depicted, promised him the kingship, provided he freed the sphinx from the sand that encumbered it. The Late Period and the Graeco-Roman era saw the spread of the practice of incubation (sleeping in the temple) in sanatoriums, which supposedly summoned up dreams and encounters with deities.

Nightmares were treated like a disease; a demon was considered the cause, and the person who was tormented by bad dreams tossed about in bed like someone with a fever. The preserved incantations against nightmares did not serve to prevent them, rather, they were used when the dreamer felt urgently threatened by these images. The treatment included protective rituals that were performed over the patient or in the bedroom. To give one example: "The book to drive off terrors that might befall a man during the night, until it is seen that (the man) is quiet," was recited over a depiction of the night barque of the sun and its magic-filled crew—by invoking this analogy (see **Question 40**), the gods would protect the sleeper at night, just as they protected the sun god. According to another text (Ostracon Gardiner 363), four clay Uraeus serpents, which were supposed to spit fire at the demons, were to be placed in the four corners of the bedroom. To this prophylactic end, the windows of the house were also to be smeared with salve, a practice that can be compared with the marking of the entrances of houses against the angel of death in the biblical story of the slaughter of Pharaoh's and Egypt's firstborn. In another ritual, the parts of the house into which danger could penetrate were identified with deities or with animals that were manifestations of deities (see **Question 45**) that would then prevent any dangers from coming into the house:

NN (the name of the patient), born of NN (the name of his mother) has conjured the window—it is a tomcat; NN, born of NN, has conjured the crack—it is a female falcon; NN, born of NN, has conjured the doorbolts—they are Ptah; NN, born of NN, has conjured the hole (for the doorbolt)—it is Nehebkau; NN, born of NN, has conjured the living room—it is He-with-the-hidden-name; NN, born of NN, has conjured his place, his room, his bed. (Pap. Chester-Beatty VIII)

44.

Could the dead read?

While this question might at first seem unusual, it is important to understand that in ancient Egypt the dead were called "the living ones," reflecting the idea that once in the afterlife the deceased continued to "live" as they had on earth. Truly "dead," in the modern sense of the word, referred only to those people who had failed to pass the Judgment of the Dead (see also **Question 39**) and, as a consequence, suffered a second and ultimate death. Funerary literature informs us of Egyptian concepts of the world beyond in which "the living ones" found themselves upon death. This literature, such as the Pyramid Texts, the Coffin Texts, the various guides to the afterlife, and the Book of the Dead, was written on the walls of tombs and coffins or on papyri that were placed in the tomb along with the deceased at the funeral. Some of these texts were recited at the funeral, but their placement in the tomb context indicates that all were meant to be utilized by the deceased in the afterlife. The deceased had, however, probably studied them while still alive, so that in the afterlife they could be confident in their ability to employ the correct spells.

All these compositions were essentially magical texts (see also **Question 40**) that provided the deceased with help, material provisions, and orientation. This was needed because the institutions and behaviors that had safeguarded the deceased in this life—cult, legal institutions, ethical conduct, social solidarity, medicine—would no longer apply in the world beyond. The afterlife was an unknown, mysterious realm, where orientation was difficult, exact knowledge was demanded, and many life-threatening dangers awaited the deceased in his or her solitude. In the Book of the Dead, its purpose is formulated thus:

> For the permanence of Osiris [every deceased became Osiris with death], giving breath to the Inert One [an epithet of Osiris] in the presence of Thoth [the god of knowledge], and repelling the enemies of Osiris when he has arrived there [the hereafter] in his various shapes; (to provide) safeguarding, protection and defense. Thoth himself has made (the book) in order that the sunlight might rest on him (the deceased) every day.

The protection of the deceased in the life beyond and the full functioning of their bodies were of utmost importance, particularly because for the ancient Egyptians there were very genuine perils in the underworld. Already in the Pyramid Texts, "dangerous" hieroglyphs (animals and men) were mutilated so that they would not come to life and eat the offerings. Other incantations were directed against snakes and scorpions, against Apopis, the enemy of the sun, against the "Donkey Swallower," crocodiles, and the gigantic trap net that stretched between sky and earth. Only an exact knowledge of the topography of the netherworld, its dangers, and the places and names of its inhabitants afforded a certain guarantee of survival in this place. Additionally, this knowledge served the deceased as a *passe-partout*, or type of "master key." Knowledge of all important entities and their names conferred power and authority over them. Thus we see in the very first spell of the Book of the Dead that the deceased establishes his legitimacy by personally identifying himself with Thoth, the god of wisdom, and by emphasizing that he has knowledge of the mysterious things that happened with regard to Osiris. It was important to know the gateways of the afterlife and their guardians, the fourteen mounds of the realm of the dead, the souls of the sacred places, the tribunal, and the Lake of Fire and its guardians. One spell, in particular, prevents the deceased from forgetting his name (and thus his identity and self-control!), while another provides for illumination, should the sun and the moon prove lacking. Other spells aim at problem-free access and freedom of movement in the realm of the dead, passage in the sun barque, and acceptance among the gods of the underworld. Yet another theme of the funerary texts is the special ability of the deceased to turn himself into many different gods, such as the creator god Atum, Osiris, and Horus, but also into other entities in the world, such as a falcon, a swallow, a snake, a crocodile, fire, air, grain, or a lotus blossom. As if surviving the outward perils of the underworld were not enough, the funerary texts also demonstrate that material provisioning had to be assured. It was a concern of several spells that in the "topsy-turvy" world of death, the digestive process itself was not to be reversed!

Armed with his papyrus roll—that is, with Thoth's book of magical spells whose very recitation assured the efficacy of the conjuration—or by reciting the texts on the walls of his tomb, the deceased acted like a veritable magician. But even more reliable than taking in knowledge by reading was what we find in the story of the magician Setne-Khaemwese, who soaked a magic book with beer, dissolved it in water and drank it, "so that he might know all that it contained."

45.

Why did the Egyptians worship animals?

M any Roman writers, including Cicero, Pliny the Elder, and Juvenal, expressed disgust at the strange (in their eyes) Egyptian worship of animals or the animal form of Egyptian deities. As Clement of Alexandria wrote:

> But if you enter the penetralia of the enclosure, and, in haste to behold something better, seek the image that is the inhabitant of the temple, and if any priest of those that offer sacrifice there, looking grave, and singing a paean in the Egyptian tongue, remove a little of the veil to show the god, he will give you a hearty laugh at the object of worship. For the deity that is sought, to whom you have rushed, will not be found within, but a cat, or a crocodile, or a serpent of the country, or some such beast unworthy of the temple, but quite worthy of a den, a hole, or the dirt. The god of the Egyptians appears a beast rolling on a purple couch.

Clement seems to be referring to divine images whose animal form symbolized an aspect of the deity, or one of his or her possible forms of manifestation.

This misperception of Egyptian gods continued into the nineteenth century when the most famous German poet and writer, Johann Wolfgang von Goethe, ridiculed the "dog-headed gods" of Egypt for being called great. He probably had in mind a scene of the Greek satirist Lucian who, in *The Gods in Council*, made the god of ridicule, Momus, deride Anubis, the

Egyptian dog-headed god of the dead, since a barking creature could not possibly be a god. Zeus' wise response that a hidden mystery might lie behind the animal form is rejected by Momus as nonsense. In another satire, *Zeus Tragoedus*, Zeus has the gods seat themselves according to the value of their metal (that is, of their statues), and Poseidon, who is made of paltry bronze, must, to his displeasure, accept the fact that the "dog-faced Egyptian," of pure gold with a golden snout, is sitting two rows in front of him. Lucian passes over the fact that the Egyptians themselves did not believe that these animal forms were the actual appearance of the gods, but rather understood them as manifestations symbolizing their individual qualities. Thus, Anubis' jackal head indicated his sovereignty over the cemeteries located in the desert, the habitat of jackals. As a hieroglyph, the jackal recumbent on a shrine denoted the expression "guardian of the mysteries," indicating that he could be regarded as the god of secret rituals. Similarly, the falcon, ruler of the sky, was a possible manifestation of the celestial god Horus. The ibis head of Thoth, god of wisdom, symbolizes his all-encompassing knowledge—the hieroglyph of the ibis pecking up food from the ground served as the writing for a verb meaning "to find, discover, diagnose." The classical writers misunderstood cultural symbols that were in no way intended to bring ridicule on the divine.

From the New Kingdom on, certain individual animals were understood to be a manifestation of the divine power (*ba* in the Egyptian language) of a god, especially a creator god, in this world. Thus, the revered Apis bull at Memphis was a manifestation of the god Ptah, and the ram of Mendes was the earthly "effective agent" of the gods Re, Shu, Geb, and Osiris—that is, of the male lineage of the Heliopolitan doctrine of creation. He could thus be represented as a four-headed ram, and four rams make their appearance in the ritual of Mendes. At death, these animals were deified and their mummies were laid to rest in catacombs. From the reign of Amenhotep III on, the Apis bull was buried at Saqqara in a funeral ceremony attended by hundreds of thousands of the faithful. In the first millennium BCE, the dead Apis bull, still buried at Saqqara, became identified with Osiris, and was an important oracle god with the name Osirapis.

The theology behind the phenomenon of sacred animals, which was sometimes derived from zoological observations, was in many cases multifaceted and complex. A case in point is that of the baboons. Groups of hamadryas baboons, which interact loudly on the rock where they sleep in the morning and evening, were for this reason represented as adorants and assistants of the sun god—for example, twenty-four stone baboons sit on the frieze above the entrance to the Great Temple of Abu Simbel. But the baboon was also understood as a manifestation of the royal ancestor god, of the primeval gods of Hermopolis, of the gods Thoth and Khonsu (as moon gods), and of Hapi, the protective god of the entrails of a mummified body. Colonies of sacred baboons were dedicated to Thoth at Hermopolis and to Ptah at Saqqara, where there was even a baboon that gave oracles, called "Baboon with the speaking face."

On the eve of the Amarna Period, we find for the first time the worship of any and all animals of a species, as opposed to specific individual animals identified by priests and installed in their special rank as the animal form of a particular deity. From the New Kingdom into the Late Period, there evolved the "mass production" of mummies of sacred animals bred in places of pilgrimage. As a result, mummified cats, ibises, falcons, crocodiles, and many other animals were sold to pilgrims as votive objects and entombed by the tens of thousands in subterranean catacombs. However, recent studies of some of these votive mummies have demonstrated that demand eventually outdid the supply—many of the wrappings contained only parts of the animal, or even a different animal entirely!

Figure 10: Ramesses II receives the insignia of his reign (crook and frail) and countless years of reign and jubilees (repetitions of his reign) from Amun-Re and Mut, in the presence of their son Khonsu (the sacred triad of gods worshipped at Karnak). Karnak temple

46.

Why was the death of the king seen as dangerous?

As the Egyptians conceived it, the king was successor to the god Horus on the throne of Egypt, and as such, the indispensable guarantor of the continued existence of the land. Rank and office distinguished him from the rest of society and elevated him above a merely human existence (Figure 10). Though not a "true" god, the king possessed divine traits, and was at least semi-divine. He was also responsible for sustaining and securing Egypt each day. According to the ritual performed by the king each morning, the sun god placed the king on earth to put *Maat* into effect and abolish chaos (see **Question 39**). Without him, the order created at the beginning of the world could not occur. The king thus acted within a defined role to which he was cultically bound. While the reasons for and goals of the king's actions were predetermined, he did have control over how he carried out this program.

Since the king was the guarantor of world order, his death threatened the world with doom. To avoid this, his successor created the world anew with his accession, and once again symbolically united Upper and Lower Egypt. The first military expedition of many a king, or his representation as a military leader even when he never made such an expedition, is to be understood in this context. The well-known Battle of Megiddo in the first year of the sole reign of Thutmose III, which he fought against an alleged coalition of 330 foreign chieftains, is a prime example of this point. The discrepancy between the size of the coalition and the amount of the booty, as well as the three-month siege needed to take the city of Megiddo, indicate that the official account of this battle derived in large part from the requirements of ideology and did not necessarily correspond to historical reality (see **Question 76**). Hymns celebrating the coronation of Merneptah and Ramesses IV depict the inception of the King's reign as the beginning of a tranquil era. The new King was enthroned, and soon, refugees returned home, the hungry were sated, the thirst of the parched was quenched, the naked were clothed, and the quarreling were peaceful, wrong was overcome and *Maat* was restored. Political tracts of the Middle Kingdom, with their very description of rulerless periods, emphasize the institution of kingship as guarantor of wellbeing (see also **Question 37**).

 **47.**

Why was there no pig
deity in ancient Egypt?

In the official religion of Egypt, the pig was demonized as unclean and as the animal of the god Seth, who could be represented as a pig and whom we see depicted in porcine form being harpooned by Horus at the temple of Edfu. Yet texts and archaeological evidence show that pigs were definitely raised, offered, and eaten (for instance, in the temple of Seti I at Abydos); they also served as a natural "garbage disposer," for example, in the workmen's settlement at Amarna. Moreover, the lone statuette of a pig deity from the late Predynastic Period shows that this animal was not always the object of religious taboo. Similarly, the (wild) donkey, which was a royal animal elsewhere in the Near East—Jesus rode into Jerusalem on a donkey—was also demonized and connected with Seth. But donkey burials, which were recently discovered in the Early Dynastic royal cemetery of Abydos, show that as with the pig this was due to a specific religious selection, not a general prohibition.

There were also other animals which, for various reasons, found little or no admittance into the religious universe of Egypt. Of the large fauna of Africa, only the hippopotamus, the mightiest inhabitant of the Nile valley, received religious adoration. The female hippopotamus was especially prominent in the prehistoric era and later in the form of the goddess Taweret (Thoeris), a birth goddess. In contrast, the male hippopotamus was negatively valued, and like the pig, seen as an animal of Seth and often the object of Horus' spear. Other examples of large fauna, such as the elephant and the giraffe, must have been too rarely attested in the environs of Egypt even at the beginning of Egyptian history to have been assigned a religious role. The same fate also befell animals that entered Egypt too late, as for example the horse, first attested in the sixteenth century BCE, or the camel, known only from 1200 BCE on. Among the predatory cats, the importance of the lion by far overshadowed that of the leopard, the cheetah, and the wild cat. There were also important regional distinctions—in the Delta city of Mendes, for instance, an ancient fish or dolphin goddess by the name Hatmehit was venerated, a goddess who was otherwise unimportant.

 **48.**

Why did the Egyptians mummify their dead?

In the modern public consciousness, scarcely any ancient Egyptian phenomenon looms as large as mummification. Egyptian mummies are a common motif in popular culture, though often in ways that are alien or false in comparison to ancient realities. Today, in fact, mummies are an essential source for our knowledge of living conditions and illnesses (see **Question 97**). Egyptology and medicine closely collaborate in investigating Egyptian mummies, using noninvasive methods and virtual digital reconstructions.

Our earliest evidence for mummification techniques dates back to the middle of the fourth millennium (late Naqada I and Naqada II cultures) at Hierakonpolis, where the head, the neck, and the hands of many bodies were protected by linen padding and partially bandaged. This was not standard practice, however, as we have contemporary Upper Egyptian burials that display a custom of disarticulating the body, mostly by removing the head, the lower arms, or the hands and placing them separately in the grave. Sometimes, these same body parts from various individuals were grouped together or piled in a heap. Finally, after 3000 BCE, the idea of preserving the whole physical body, not just the parts of immediate relevance for taking nourishment and breathing, became the obligatory burial custom for the king and the elite (see also **Question 12**). We must note, though, that mummification was always a form of burial restricted to those who could afford it, even though the percentage of the population who had themselves mummified increased considerably over time, down into the

Graeco-Roman Period (see **Question 88**). Despite this increase, mummification was not the funerary practice of the majority of the Egyptian population—in all periods, most Egyptians were buried without any artificial treatment that would preserve the body, and were often merely placed in simple pits in the sand.

The technically complicated process of mummification, which was accompanied by ritual activities—from the cleansing of the body through the removal of the brain and the internal organs, the desiccation of the body in natron, the restitution of the body's original appearance, the actual embalming and bandaging of the corpse, the insertion of amulets, and, finally, the mummification of the internal organs—demanded the emergence of a specialized group of professionals. As described by the Greek historian Herodotus, Egyptians could choose between three types of mummification, each of which differed in cost, and then, after death, the body was entrusted to the embalmers and the funerary priests responsible for the area of the cemeteries where the tomb was located. While funerary religion had been the original reason for the emergence of mummification, it gradually became a lucrative and major economic sector. By the first millennium BCE, this mummification economy used older tombs of the third and second millennia, for example at Saqqara, for secondary burials that in many cases filled the chambers right up to their ceilings.

The Middle Ages witnessed the awakening of a pharmaceutical interest in Egyptian mummies, at first in Islamic and then European medicine. These corpses, hardened into a black, tar-like mass by the embalming process, looked like bitumen, which had been prized as a curative ever since classical antiquity. It was for this reason that the word *mumiya*, "bitumen," which passed from the Persian language into Arabic, became the designation of these Egyptian bodies. In the modern period, there developed a trade in mummies to supply the apothecaries of Europe, where "genuine Egyptian mummy" (*mumia vera aegyptiaca*) was sold as a medicine as late as the nineteenth century. A famous witness to this usage was the "Lübeck Apothecary Mummy" in Germany, which was on display from

1696 in a pharmacy in the city of Lübeck in northern Germany. It is the body of a 40-year-old man who died around 600 BCE, and wrapped into the mummy were no fewer than sixty-two amulets to protect the deceased (see also **Question 51**).

 **49.**

To whom were flowers given in ancient Egypt?

In ancient Egyptian the words for "floral bouquet" and "life" were identical (*ankh*), thus bouquets of flowers not only symbolized, but even brought about, new life. The deceased received bouquets from deities (that is, wreaths that were dedicated in the temple of the deity in question and then purchased), while funerary texts tell us that the deceased received wreaths after successfully undergoing the Judgment of the Dead (see also **Question 39**). There were wreaths of flowers lying on the sarcophagus of Tutankhamun when it was discovered in 1922 by Howard Carter, and in the deposit of embalming material found in the Valley of the Kings in 2005 (KV 64), there was a whole coffin filled with floral garlands and wreaths. This already shows that flowers, which the dead wanted to receive as donations from the living, were consecrated and cultic objects whose effects were viewed as equal to those of amulets (see **Question 51**). In an episode from the Late Period Papyrus Vandier, the magician Merire volunteers to die instead of his doomed pharaoh, and he enters into the netherworld. After the goddess Hathor tells him that the King, at the instigation of the court magicians, has violated the oath he had sworn not to lay hands on Merire's family, he creates an artificial man out of mud—a golem—who wreaks vengeance on the scheming magicians. Having done his duty, this golem brings a floral bouquet to Merire in the netherworld. Finally, in depictions, a bouquet could even take the place of the deceased, representing not only eternal life, but also the fragrance that emanated from the deified dead.

Pleasant fragrance was in fact viewed as a divine quality. When the god Amun approached Queen Hatshepsut's mother in the guise of her husband, Thutmose I, "the palace was filled with divine fragrance." Especially important, then, was the flowers' scent (one term for flower was "fragrance of the garden")—for instance, that of the blooms of the blue lotus, pomegranate, jasmine, Christ's-thorn, various herbs, and henna, which were all pungent. When Psammetichus II campaigned in Syria in 592 BCE, he brought along various priests carrying bouquets in which, as scholars have suggested, the gods were believed present in the fragrance of their respective flower. But flowers were also bound together into victory wreaths (after successful military campaigns), and employed as gifts, decorations, and symbols of life on the occasion of festivals, processions, and banquets. According to the account of the reign of Ramesses III in the Great Papyrus Harris, the god Amun received, as "other offerings," the enormous figures of 60,450 wreaths, 620 containers (of flowers), 12,400 blue flowers threaded on strings, 46,500 "handfuls" of flowers, and 110 heaps of flowers.

50.

Why did Egyptian religion need foreign gods?

In every period, Egypt had extensive knowledge of the neighboring civilizations of Africa and the Levant, though only bits and pieces of this knowledge have survived to us. It surely included knowledge of foreign religions, which would have been acquired through trade, diplomacy, military and quarrying expeditions, as well as foreign immigrants. The earliest foreign god we know of, who appears in the Pyramid Texts, is the Syrian star god Ashtar, and by around 1700 BCE at the latest, the Levantine storm god Baal was venerated in Egypt. Our knowledge of foreign religious influence is limited by the hazards of preservation, by the selectivity of the sources—many foreign deities appear only in magical papyri—and by our fragmentary knowledge of certain social and professional milieus—for instance, the lower class and the military. In this regard, it is also important to note that the borders between Egypt and foreign territories shifted during the course of history (see also **Question 70**). Until around 2000 BCE, the Delta east of the Pelusiac branch of the Nile was not a part of Egypt and was viewed as foreign soil, and it remained an area of cultural exchange between Egypt and Palestine. The protective deity of the southeast Delta, the Sinai, and the Red Sea coast was the god Sopdu, who was represented as an Asiatic. Similarly diffuse was the situation in the western Delta, which was a transitional area to Libya and Libyan culture, and where the "Libyan Goddess" was worshiped. Egypto-Libyan gods of this border area were Ash and Ha, the latter being lord of the western desert and also a protective god of the dead, as we learn from coffins of the Herakleopolitan Period from Siut. In the south, the First Cataract, which was the area bordering on Nubia, was a similar transitional zone, home to the Nubian-Egyptian god Dedwen. But the narrow Nile valley itself was bordered immediately by the foreign territories which the Eastern and Western deserts represented. In this vein, the fertility god Min of Koptos was thus also the patron of the desert trails that led from Koptos to the Red Sea, and he was called "the Nubian of the Eastern desert." Colossal statues of Min dating back to the end of the fourth millennium BCE are decorated with sawfish and mussels representing the fauna of the Red Sea. Conversely, by way of an *interpretatio aegyptiaca*, foreign goddesses from the Lebanon all the way to Nubia and even Punt, the land of incense on the Red Sea coast, were identified with the Egyptian goddess Hathor.

During the New Kingdom a number of foreign deities entered Egypt; they evidently filled theological and ideological gaps that the traditional gods and goddesses could not adequately cover. An essential role in this process seems to have been played by the reorganization of the Egyptian army after the introduction of the horse and chariot. In the Ramesside Residence of Qantir/Pi-Ramesses in the eastern Nile Delta, a temple was dedicated to the goddess Astarte, who, as a goddess of war, served as patroness of the king's team of horses (see also **Question 58** and the hymn of praise about Pi-Ramesses cited there). Similarly, the Levantine Anat, well known as a violent warrior, was a protective goddess of the Egyptian king in war. But the deity chosen to be the actual patron of a new military kingship and protective god of the Ramesside royal family around 1300 BCE was the Syrian storm god Baal, who in Egypt also received the name Seth because of the similar nature of the two deities. From this time also comes our earliest preserved Late Egyptian tale, which relates how Seth/Baal, assisted by the goddess Astarte, saves the world from a devastating flood. About a century earlier, under Amenhotep II, we find mention of other deities in Egypt who provided protection against the plague and who thus might have been introduced in connection with the epidemic that wreaked havoc in the ancient Near East at that time (see **Question 33**). Reshef, a west Semitic god of plague and war and guardian of the gate to the netherworld, was mostly depicted in a threatening pose, brandishing a battle axe or a mace above his head. Haurun, a god of the netherworld and helper against snakes and demons, was identified at Giza with the Great Sphinx, which was an image of the Egyptian god Harmakhis. While all these deities represented aspects of violence, we also find an Asiatic goddess of sexuality, fertility, and healing venerated in Thebes and elsewhere in the Ramesside Period: the goddess Qudshu who was depicted nude and fully frontal, which was very atypical in Egyptian art (see also **Question 54**).

 **51.**

Did amulets really help those who wore them?

From all periods of Egyptian history, we have hundreds of thousands of amulets, magical objects intended to provide their wearers with protection. The external appearance of these amulets is remarkably diverse, depicting everything from little divine figurines to religious symbols and animals, and even hieroglyphs. W.M.F. Petrie, who essentially founded Egyptian archaeology in the late nineteenth century, was convinced that we can derive the function of amulets from their external form. Thus, he distinguished (1) amulets intended to be effective via analogy; persons wearing a hare amulet wanted the regenerative ability of the hare (as an animal who could survive in the desert), (2) amulets in the form of power symbols (such as crowns), which could endow their wearers with that power, (3) amulets in the form of grave goods or personal possessions, which could guarantee that their wearers would have these items in the afterlife, (4) amulets in the form of symbols (*e.g.*, the *udjat*-eye), which could provide protection and ward off illness, and (5) amulets in the form of divine beings whose help was desired by those who wore them. Though classifications of this sort are made to this day, they are far too subjective to further our understanding of amulets. The decisive point is that amulets were magical objects that were hung or placed on the person who was in need of their protection, living or dead, during a ritual. Provided the ritual actions were carried out correctly and the appropriate spell was recited, the amulet fulfilled its function (see also **Question 40**).

For the most part, amulets have come down to us without instructions for how to perform the actions and which spell to recite. In many cases, it is thus scarcely possible to decide what the ancient Egyptians understood as the purpose of amulets. Fortunately, however, in a few cases, complete instructions have been preserved. They show that even when the general goal (protection and endowment with power of the living or dead person) is clear, the specific understanding of certain amulets, even if they look similar, depends on other factors (the material of which it is made, where it is to be applied, *etc.*). In the late magical Papyrus Brooklyn, for instance, we find the following instruction copied from a healing statue of Ramesses III:

> Words to be spoken over a lion of faïence, threaded onto a string of red linen. It is placed on a man's arm. It is given as protection for his bedroom. [text of the spell]: 'He [the king] is a lion who protects himself. He is the great god who fights for his brother. Who bites him will not stay alive. For he is a lion who wards off gods and ghosts. He has warded off all male and female snakes that bite with their jaws.'

Here, the lion amulet is identified with the King as a lion, whose power is thus transferred to the man who wears it. At the same time, the lion's fighting power is enhanced by the color red, which is usually associated with negative things and with the god Seth, and by a verbal association (the word for faïence, *tjehenet*, sounds the same as the verb *tjehen*, "to meet someone in battle").

We find an entirely different constellation in the case of the lion amulet of Coffin Text spell 83:

> Words to be spoken over the forepart of a lion, to be made from carnelian or vulture bone and to be placed on a man's neck when he descends to the necropolis. A protection in the form of the Ba of the god Shu. This means: A man's sway over the winds of the sky, to become one endowed with effective magic and to become king of

all winds of the sky. He cannot die again, his enemies cannot take possession of him, and sorcery on earth (black magic!) will not be able to hold him back.

Here, an identification with the *ba*—that is, the powerful manifestation of Shu, god of the air—is achieved through the form of the amulet, the material of which it is made, and its application to the neck. According to Coffin Text spell 75, Shu has more magical power than Heka, the god of magic himself. The two spells also show that not only the form of the amulet, but also its qualities, its color, and its designation, are of decisive importance. An Egyptian patient most likely had little knowledge of how precisely the amulet worked, yet he still trusted in its efficacy. This is not unlike patients today who understand little of the science behind modern medicine but nonetheless believe that the drug administered will work.

 # 52.

Why do we speak of the "hiddenness of myth" in ancient Egypt?

Compared to the Graeco-Roman world, elaborate narrative myths appeared late in the history of Egypt, and often, they are outright unattested, thus seeming intentionally "hidden." The most important Egyptian myth, that of Osiris, Isis, and Horus, is first attested in continuous form in the Ptolemaic temple of Edfu and in the writings of the Greek philosopher Plutarch (46–129 CE). Jan Assmann has therefore proposed that we distinguish two types of myth: the "genotype" of a myth as an abstract complex of concepts regarding specific deities, and the "phenotype" as an actual mythic statement or an individual mythic narrative that chooses a specific perspective out of the entire complex and is fixed as such in writing. For example, many allusions, episodes, or longer narratives refer to the myth of Isis and Osiris, but prior to the Roman Period no text related the whole myth. Rather, specific aspects of the myth were written down and recited based on very concrete needs. According to Assmann, mythic statements are always either *action-related* or *knowledge-related*. In a spell against snake poison, mention is made of the mythic episode in which the Horus child was cured of a snakebite (action-related). In regard to the origin of a cult, we read a mythic episode that yields the respective reason or etiology (knowledge-related).

There is also disagreement as to whether there were myths that served as purely entertainment literature—this has been claimed, for instance, for the Late Egyptian story of Horus and Seth. The idea of goal-orientation could also apply to those myths that can be called "political myths," and which surely had an actual historical background. The text we call The Memphite Theology, inscribed on a stone slab in the British Museum, thematizes the fight of Horus and Seth over the kingship of Egypt, and the primacy of the city of Memphis and its creator god Ptah. The tale of Horus and Seth in Papyrus Chester-Beatty I could be a legitimation myth, stressing the correct line of succession to the throne which was disputed in the reign of Ramesses V. The Book of the Heavenly Cow, which relates humankind's revolt against Re and how the goddess Sakhmet attempted to annihilate the human race but was prevented from doing so by a ruse (see **Question 91**), could have been written in the context of the plague that devastated the Near East at the end of the fourteenth century BCE (see **Question 33**). The amazement of modern Egyptologists at the "hiddenness of myth" shows, incidentally, how caught up they are in the western classical perspective—the open display of Graeco-Roman myth. The Egyptian priests would have opposed this revealing of sacral information, for they considered seclusion to be the correct form of dealing with mythical knowledge (see **Question 42**).

5

Egyptian Art, Archaeology, and Architecture

Figure 11: Head of a sculpture of Senwosret III
(*c*.1850 BCE).

 **53.**

What was the purpose of ancient Egyptian art?

People create art (buildings, paintings, statues, *etc.*) to reflect and evaluate reality and as a response to their questions and needs. At the same time, art is understood as the result of human aesthetic activity transposed into objects that also convey such things as beauty, quality, and creativity. In Egyptological discussions of art, the assessment of both these points has always been of central importance. While Cyril Aldred (1949) viewed aesthetics as ancient Egypt's special contribution to the totality of artistic experience, Walter Wolf (1957) categorically disagreed, stating, "Aesthetic considerations played no role whatsoever in the origin (of an Egyptian work of art)." According to Wolf, Egyptian art works were always created to fulfill a particular function; in Egypt, an art work was not so much something artfully created, but rather an "implement," a magical "utensil" (see also **Question 19**). In her recent introduction to Egyptian art, Marie-Ange Bonhême spoke of nothing less than the "art of the magician." If we consider all the Egyptian art preserved to us, we see that it comprises a great many works of poor quality that were nevertheless functional on the magical level. In ancient Egypt, a work of art could fulfill its function only in the place for which it had been intended, in concert with other art objects (such as architecture, statuary, and reliefs in a pyramid precinct), with items alien—in our eyes—to art (such as offering tables and offerings), and with a more comprehensive religious landscape (such as the mutual arrangement and location of the Theban temples).

Since the 1980s, scholars have once again begun to emphasize the aesthetic component of Egyptian art, making reference to any number of preserved ancient Egyptian statements praising the beauty of a temple or the splendid execution of a statue. The beauty of their art was thus important to the Egyptians, who took note of it and prized it. Scholars assumed that this aesthetic perfection also meant that art was not intended to represent something individual, but rather something ideal—the ideal human, not the actual person; the world as a universal, not the actual world around us. But would the work of art not have been an instrument of magic even so? Moreover, innumerable statues and depictions are most surely individual, from the bust of Prince Ankhhaf in Dynasty 4 to that of Monthemhet, mayor of Thebes around 650 BCE (cf. Figure 11).

John Baines has stressed that an important criterion of art—a public—definitely existed in Egypt: first of all, the elite person who commissioned the art work, and then the gods, but also society in general. High quality not only assured the ritual effectiveness of the work of art, it also guaranteed the satisfaction of the one who commissioned it (and thus, potentially, allowed the artist a share in his afterlife), and gave the artist social status and recognition. Additionally, art also served to define the social status of the state elite. The elite distinguished themselves from the lower social strata through their control over art, its forms of expression, and the resources necessary to create it. Art meant cultural knowledge, as did the hieroglyphic writing system, and luxury as well. Art also conveyed identity and legitimation, which in turn led to its increased valorization.

 **54.**

Does Egyptian art speak to us?

Egyptian art strikes us today as genuinely "Egyptian," in particular specific features of how humans and deities are depicted: the body is shown in profile, but with a frontal depiction of the torso, and mostly two identically depicted hands. The purpose of this artistic convention was not to truthfully render what the human eye saw, but to display a body that was as complete and functional as needed and not disfigured by the eye's perspective. In the same vein, objects and structures are displayed with the aim of showing their enduring nature and most significant features—so, for example, the side and top view of a stool could be combined into one picture as could the top view of a garden with side views of the birds in the garden's pool and the plants surrounding it. This schematic (rather than naturalistic) depiction is also the case with the canon of proportions used for human figures. Until the 26th Dynasty, the standard canon used a grid of eighteen squares up to the hairline (nineteen squares to the top of the head), irrespective of whether their true appearance would have corresponded to this ideal (see also **Question 86**). The schematic nature of Egyptian art is also visible in the convention of depicting more important individuals as taller than less important ones.

It seems clear that this "language" of Egyptian art is both peculiar to and a reflection of the Egyptian world view. Thus it should not be seen as inferior to our western artistic conventions, but needs to be properly understood—and contextualized—to be given justice. How does this go together with some modern ideas about Egyptian art? The Italian

Egyptologist Sergio Donadoni has expressed the opinion that it "is legitimate to read works of Egyptian art directly, to consider them in conjunction with one another, to understand them as an organic web of experiences that stands at our disposal in a perpetual simultaneity that enables it to express itself through itself. Art can often do without commentary, needing only to be accepted in its essential simplicity." Writing about statues of the Old Kingdom, the German scholar Dietrich Wildung has stated, "In an exemplary manner, detailed art historical consideration of royal sculpture supplies insights into basic ideological and political processes, testifying to the role of the work of art as a primary source for history. Art as direct language of its time: no other medium makes it possible, in the way that the art of ancient Egypt does, to resurrect the living reality of the third millennium BCE."

It must be pointed out, however, that Old Kingdom art can be viewed as the "language of its time" mostly because contemporary written sources do not yet exist; it is a highly problematic matter to draw conclusions about history from individual aspects of art. It is equally tricky to try to read Egyptian art directly or to accept it in its alleged simplicity. These objects do not state their purpose, rather, it has to be inferred from their original context—for instance, whether a statue is from a temple, or a tomb context. In addition, we have only a very partial and rudimentary understanding of the iconic signs Egyptian works of art employ—for example, the types of representation, clothing, attributes, pose, gestures, and so forth. Like language (see **Questions 71** and **72**), art is a system of symbols that a society has agreed upon to make a statement, and we are far removed from the ancient Egyptians who conceived of this system. It thus seems unduly simplistic to assert that this symbolic system can, after the passage of millennia, speak directly to the beholder (and not just make an aesthetic impression)—by way of an example, we can seldom decipher the reasons why the Egyptian king wears specific crowns or headdresses in certain scenes, but not in others.

55.

What is ancient Egypt's most important architectural monument?

There are several possible answers to this question. If we consider religious architecture, then the funerary complex of King Djoser of Dynasty 3 (c.2700 BCE) at Saqqara, with its step pyramid, is the most important architectural monument, both architectonically and from the point of view of cultural history. Even two and a half millennia later, Djoser himself and his architect Imhotep, who in the first millennium BCE was deified and identified with Asclepius, the Greek god of healing, were considered to be the inventors of stone architecture and were seen as cultural heroes. Although stone architecture had its precursors, and Djoser's complex was constructed in the context of the existing religious landscape of Saqqara, which included Dynasty 2 royal tombs and elite monumental mudbrick mastaba tombs of Dynasty 1, it was, in its totality, without precedent in Egypt. It exerted a determining influence on the later architectonic and theological development of royal funerary architecture. Djoser was the first Egyptian king not to have a tomb at Abydos in Upper Egypt. Instead, in addition to his actual burial chamber beneath the Step Pyramid, there was a ritual "southern tomb" within his pyramid complex. With his decision to elevate the mastaba, a simple stone "bench," into a loftier, six-stepped pyramid, Djoser was responsible for the choice of the pyramid as the principal form of Egyptian royal funerary architecture. But the complex also signaled the rise of divine kingship, which needed a monumental form of expression that would visually dominate the Nile valley. The emphasis on the burial chamber, at the expense of storerooms, lent expression to the belief that the divine king no longer had need of direct provisioning with actual grave goods. This burial chamber, unique in being accessible only through its ceiling, rested on pillars, perhaps symbolizing the placement of the grave in the primeval ocean that lay beneath the earth, and in which the King was regenerated. Surrounding the rock core, a complex of galleries decorated with relief carvings of mats and false doors might have represented the King's palace in the next life, through whose gates the King would stride eastward into the land of the living to participate in the cult. Above ground, the layout of the complex could also have served the eternal sovereignty of the deceased King over the cosmos, and allowed for his participation in cults and festival celebrations. This complex consisted of large-scale chapels (the court with Upper and Lower Egyptian chapels was perhaps a depiction in stone of the geography of Egypt), a court for cultic runs of the King, and a rich program of statuary. Even eighty years after the initial excavation of the complex, Djoser's funerary enclosure has not yet been fully investigated, nor is its significance truly understood.

But if we were to choose, out of all the architecture that survives to us, the one edifice that in and of itself offers the most information for our modern understanding of Egypt, then we would probably have to name the temple of Edfu. The best preserved temple from all antiquity, it was built and decorated between 237 and 57 BCE. Its walls, totaling about a kilometer in length, are covered with a huge array of texts that comprise a veritable compendium of Egypt's religious tradition. The publication of the inscriptions alone fills fifteen volumes (including 3,000 pages printed with hieroglyphs); to this date, fewer than half of these texts have been studied and translated. Like the texts from other late temples, they are of central importance, for they include the content of older religious writings: texts informing us of priestly duties and temple cult, the coronation of the king and the installation of the sacred falcon of Edfu, a detailed version of the Horus myth (see **Question 52**), New Year's hymns and protective rituals, various creation myths, and even a list of the temple's landed properties (important for the study of temple economy), as well as many more.

The Great Pyramid of Giza, counted as one of the Seven Wonders of the World in classical antiquity and today the most famous monument of Egypt, is important from yet another point of view. More than any other single work of architecture, it kept the memory of Egyptian civilization alive through the ages and epitomizes the recollection and reception of Egypt in western civilization—an important starting point for the modern scientific rediscovery of Egypt (see also **Question 8**).

56.

What is the most important excavation of the last half century?

Every excavation, past and present, contributes (often decisively) to a better understanding of Egypt. If we focus on excavations that not only deepen existing knowledge, but also reveal hitherto entirely unknown areas of Egyptian culture and thus have led to a genuine change in our perspective, then the most important excavation of the last half century has surely been the recovery of Avaris/Tell el-Dab'a in the eastern Nile Delta, the capital of the Hyksos during the Second Intermediate Period. Not only is Tell el-Dab'a now the most thoroughly studied site in the Nile Delta, a region of which our knowledge remains so fragmentary (see **Question 20**), it is also a prime example of a mixed culture in a border region of Egypt. As such, it has changed our understanding of the entire second millennium, the period when Avaris and its successor city, Pi-Ramesses/Qantir, were two of ancient Egypt's capitals. Excavated by Manfred Bietak and the Austrian Archaeological Institute, this project is also one of the most thoroughly and exemplarily published excavations to date.

Avaris/Tell el-Dab'a was initially laid out as a planned settlement on the Pelusiac branch of the Nile as part of the internal colonization of Egypt that took place during the early Middle Kingdom (see **Question 31**). Throughout the Middle Kingdom the city continuously grew because of a state-supported influx of soldiers and specialized craftsmen. Almost from the beginning, the evidence for religion, burial customs, and architecture demonstrates that Egyptian and Palestinian culture existed side by side. It was this Egypto-Palestinian city that served its acculturated elite as a base when it rose to kingship after the collapse of Dynasty 13. As the new rulers of the north, called Hyksos (*ḥḳȝ ḫȝswt*, "rulers of foreign lands"), they displayed ethnic traits of Levantine culture even as they observed the ideological and cultural traditions of Egyptian kingship (see **Question 32**). With the eventual defeat of the Hyksos, the kings of Dynasty 18 maintained the city as a military base and local capital. From the reign of Thutmose III, Minoan frescoes are attested at Avaris, one of the singular finds for which this site has become famous.

Of comparable importance for our understanding of Egyptian urban culture is Elephantine, located on Egypt's southern border with Nubia. Ongoing systematic excavations by the German and Swiss Archaeological Institutes are resulting in the reconstruction of the history of this city with a precision and comprehensiveness that is unparalleled elsewhere.

 # 57.

Did early Egyptian art come from Mesopotamia?

Decorative palettes and engraved knife handles of the late fourth millennium BCE include a number of motifs found in the predynastic art of early Mesopotamia—that is, from Sumer and Elam. The best-known example is the Gebel el-Arak knife, with its depiction of a lion tamer with a long skirt, a full beard, and a cap. The knife handle is also decorated with animals with stylized folds of skin, and with skirmishes on land and on water involving bald-headed men and men with braided hair. Intertwined snakes decorated with rosettes appear on a number of knife handles, as they do in Elam, where they symbolize the presence of game animals and the suppression of chaos. Also as in Elam, some Egyptian knife handles and a mace from Nubia depict the animal bodies divided into segments. We often see the Mesopotamian motif of the griffin or winged dragon, as on the knife in the Brooklyn Museum, with its rows of animals totaling 227 in number. Recent finds of at least six more decorated knife handles and a nearly complete knife from the Predynastic cemetery of Umm el-Qaab at Abydos demonstrate that the Gebel el-Arak handle, often claimed to be a forgery, is indeed authentic. What we encounter here, and in comparable depictions, such as the "master of animals" from the famous painted tomb 100 of a ruler at Hierakonpolis, is the intentional use of motifs with known meaning in a new—Egyptian—context, and thus, a transmission of ideas.

Such transmissions might also have played an important role in the invention of the Egyptian writing system (see **Question 71**) and in the appearance of certain technological innovations. To give some examples: niched architecture made its first appearance in Egypt in Dynasty 1 (the so-called "Menes tomb" at Naqada) and was later executed in stone (*e.g.*, in the Djoser complex), but has no precursors in Egypt, while in Mesopotamia, niched walls are attested as early as the sixth millennium BCE. The recovery of niches on the interior side of a wall in an early grave at Minshat Abu Omar in the eastern Delta, however, has pointed to the possibility that there are gaps in the preserved evidence in Egypt. Brick architecture is first attested in Egypt in the Naqada II era, when it makes a sudden appearance in fully developed form, whereas in western Asia, we can observe a development of mud brick architecture that began in the eighth millennium BCE. The problems for scholars also become clear from the discovery at Buto in the Nile Delta of what are allegedly clay pegs like those inserted into the plasterwork of temple and palace walls in Mesopotamia of the Uruk Period, where they served as wall decorations and coverings (peg mosaics), or as fastenings for other decorative elements. For this reason, archaeologists postulated that the early structure at Buto was decorated according to Mesopotamian prototypes, an indication of cultural influence from Sumer and Elam. This interpretation has, however, been called into question by several scholars. Thus, while it is possible to say that the Egyptians evidently borrowed ideological motifs from Mesopotamia during the Naqada II era (*c*.3300 BCE), the transfer of technological knowledge (brick architecture, niched decoration, peg mosaics, writing) stands in need of further confirmation.

Was ancient Egypt a civilization without cities?

Cities are defining features of human civilization, and the connection between urban culture and civilization is deeply rooted in western thought. While scholars have long viewed Graeco-Roman antiquity as an urban world, Egyptology has been largely preoccupied by the "problem" of cities in ancient Egypt. The problem here was the missing evidence for (not the absence of) cities—the important cities were either not preserved or unexcavated. Nonetheless, we have learned that in Egypt, as elsewhere in the Near East at the end of the fourth millennium BCE, the development of cities and the emergence of statehood were closely connected. As centers of trade, economy, and technology, of services, culture, and social stratification, cities were the focal points of political power. In the course of Egyptian history, they took on many forms, from small towns with a few hundred inhabitants to metropolises foreshadowing those of the later classical world. Egyptian hymns sang the praise of cities such as Memphis, Thebes, and Pi-Ramesses, sometimes in comparison to each other:

> His majesty has built himself a palace called 'The one of great Victories.' It lies between Palestine and Egypt and is full of food and nourishment. It looks like Thebes, its permanence is that of Memphis. The sun rises in its horizon and sets in its midst [an allusion to the size of the city?]. All men leave their cities and settle in its area. Its western part is the temple of Amun, its southern

the temple of Seth. Astarte dwells on the side of the sunrise, Wadjit on the northern side. The castle that lies at its center resembles the horizon of the sky [...] How beautiful it was [...] when you built Pi-Ramesses, the beginning of every foreign land and the end of Egypt, with magnificent windows and dazzling chambers of lapis lazuli and turquoise [*i.e.*, with dazzling faïence tiles in the colors of these semiprecious stones], the city where your chariot warriors are trained, the place where your infantry are trained, the place where your fleet is docked when it brings you the tribute (of foreign lands).

Whether in the Nile valley or the Delta, cities, which were built of mud brick, are badly preserved or have been leveled. Moreover, archaeologists in Egypt used to mostly concentrate their efforts on monumental stone architecture. The great metropolises of Egypt are thus all destroyed or yet to be excavated (see **Questions 20** and **56**). Memphis, which once had at least 100,000 inhabitants (see **Question 93**), lies buried under the palm groves of Saqqara; the Middle Kingdom city of Thebes was leveled to make way for the New Kingdom temple of Karnak; and while the location of the New Kingdom city is known, it has never been systematically investigated. Even the 19th Dynasty Residence of Pi-Ramesses in the eastern Delta, which covered an area of ten square kilometers, has barely begun to be explored. We must note, in this connection, that the inhabitable area of Egypt was about the size of the state of Maryland, so that for the New Kingdom, we must think in terms of only a few major cities and perhaps a few dozen smaller ones. But while we can make detailed reconstructions of the structure and functions of ancient Greek and Roman cities, this is only exceptionally possible in Egypt. A few such cases include the city of Akhetaten (Amarna), founded on virgin soil and never overbuilt in later times, which served as Akhenaten's sacred residence in Middle Egypt (see **Question 33**), or cities like Avaris and Elephantine, which have become better known through excavations conducted in recent years (see **Question 56**).

 **59.**

Why did King Snofru curtail artistic freedom?

Until early in Dynasty 4, members of the royal family and private persons enjoyed considerable autonomy in the fashioning of their tombs. For roughly the first half of the Old Kingdom, tombs took the form of large brick mastabas (tombs with a rectangular superstructure) with highly individual layouts and up to a dozen subterranean chambers. At Saqqara, the mastabas adopted many architectural elements from Djoser's royal enclosure (see **Question 56**), which served as a model. Individuals had themselves depicted in relief and in statues of stone or wood, and even appropriated the previously royal privilege of being represented standing. Standing and seated statues of the private tomb owners—in one case, a shipwright!—now guaranteed the continued existence and status that the individual had achieved in his lifetime. The increase in individuality is also made clear by the tomb reliefs, with their larger scale and richer range of themes (*e.g.*, hunting in the desert, scenes of animals), and in their execution, where artists experimented with new techniques.

From the second half of the reign of Snofru through the reign of Khufu, however, there was a drastic curtailing of this freedom, a phenomenon for which we use the term "austere style," coined by Hermann Junker. Now, in the pyramid cemeteries of Dahshur and Giza, the austere style decreed uniform rows of small, identically shaped mastabas with nothing but plain façades, "laid out around the pyramid," as Jacques Vandier has described them, "like the houses of a village." The tomb owner could be depicted only walking or seated at his offering table, while the formerly rich variety of wall representations was replaced by scenes of offering bearers—the only scene type permitted. Individualistic features of private tombs were even retroactively eliminated: the chapels of the large brick mastabas at Maidum, regardless of the high rank of their owners, were now walled up and their exterior walls plastered over, thus bringing them into line with the new canon of tomb architecture. The statues of private persons were walled up in their chapels, thus removing them from view. This practice had the fortunate side effect of resulting in the preservation of statue groups such as that of Rahotep and Nofret, now in the Cairo Museum, whose lifelike appearance—due to the amazing preservation of the paint—surprised, even startled, the discoverers.

The motives for this curtailment of the living evolution of the cult and the décor of private tombs can be seen in the development of an absolute, divine monarchy and the concept of the king as ruler in the world beyond. Cultic veneration was to be accorded exclusively to the deceased king, and not to other individuals. Likewise, the king alone was to possess decisive power over the assignment of offerings, and with that, over existence in the next life. A puzzling phenomenon from the period of the "austere style," predominantly attested at Giza, are the so-called "reserve heads," limestone heads placed between the tomb shaft and the burial chamber. Portrait-like in their execution, most have no ears, which has been ascribed by some to a curtailment of the private funerary cult: the deceased was to dwell in the head, but he could no longer hear his family members calling him to receive his offerings or return to the world above to receive their direct worship. For presumably political and ideological reasons, this curtailment of private art was rescinded in the second half of the reign of Khafre (Greek Chephren).

🦤 60.

How was the Great Pyramid built?

The question of how the pyramids—and the Great Pyramid of Khufu as the most famous one of all—were built will perhaps never be answered definitively. The problem has given rise to a huge quantity of scientific and pseudoscientific literature. If nothing else, Mark Lehner's discovery of the workers' settlement on the Giza plateau (Figure 12) has led to a clearer understanding of how the labor was organized. A total of about 12,000–15,000 workmen must have been occupied constructing the Great Pyramid, but for logistic reasons, no more than about 2,000–3,000 could have been accommodated on the construction site itself. Orientating the pyramid's sides and leveling the ground on which the pyramid was to be built (with a core of rock left in place in the case of Khufu's pyramid) was carried out with extraordinary precision, even by the standards of modern measurement techniques. The greatest difference in height between the four sides of the Khufu pyramid amounts to only two centimeters, the deviation from north to only 2°49", and the greatest error in the right angles of the corners to only fifty-eight arcseconds (and this even though, because of the rock core, there was no diagonal line of sight and thus no possibility of control across the construction site). This precision was achieved with the simplest of tools, such as the archipendulum, the plumb-bob, measuring cords and rods, and a sighting device for observing the stars. Yet in scholarship on the topic, there is no prevailing agreement as to the specific ways in which these were put to use. There are also numerous competing proposals for explaining how the stone blocks were transported up the continually growing mass of the pyramid, all having to do with various sorts of ramps—external, internal (the most recent hypothesis that still needs confirmation), running spiral fashion around the pyramid, and so forth. There are many other proposals, some of them in connection with ramps for the transport of the stone blocks to the construction site or for the pyramid core. One idea postulates levering devices lying on the individual stone layers of the pyramid prior to the placement of the casing stones. Another hypothesis posits that the stone blocks were pulled up wooden rails climbing parallel to the long sides of the core layers, with the rollers allowing those doing the pulling to exert a greater force.

Figure 12: The Great Sphinx of Giza and the pyramid of Khafre, in the foreground the Sphinx temple (*c.*2500 BCE)

 # 61.

What was the "Egyptian Labyrinth"?

S ome of the Greek and Roman writers—Herodotus, Diodorus, Strabo, Pliny—describe the temple precinct of the
pyramid of Amenemhet III at Hawara on the edge of the Faiyum
as an architectural "Wonder of the World" called the Labyrinth.
One of the last visitors of the monument was supposedly the
Roman Emperor Septimius Severus during his stay in Egypt in
199–200 CE. These classical writers must have associated the
Egyptian structure with the legendary Cretan Labyrinth of the
Minotaur; or, alternatively, they heard an Egyptian designation
that sounded similar to the Greek term "labyrinth," and then
named the structure accordingly. The layout of the structure
was unique, if we are to believe the ancient accounts, and it
even inspired scholars of the Renaissance and Baroque periods,
such as Athanasius Kircher, to attempt a reconstruction of its
appearance. Extolling the Labyrinth, Herodotus claimed that
the money and effort expended in constructing it exceeded
the sum of all the monuments of Greece, and that it even
surpassed the pyramids in grandiosity:

> It has twelve roofed courts, with doors facing one
> another [...] There are double sets of chambers in it,
> some underground and some above, and their number
> is three thousand; there are fifteen hundred of each. We
> ourselves saw the aboveground chambers, for we went
> through them [...] , but the underground chambers we
> can speak of only from hearsay. For the officials of the
> Egyptians entirely refused to show us these, saying that

there were, in them, the coffins of the kings who had builded the labyrinth at the beginning and also those of the holy crocodiles [...] The passages through the rooms and the winding goings-in and out through the courts, in their extreme complication, caused us countless marvelings as we went through, from the court into the rooms, and from the rooms into the pillared corridors, and then from these corridors into other rooms again, and from the rooms into other courts afterwards. The roof of the whole is stone, as the walls are, and the walls are full of engraved figures, and each court is set round with pillars of white stone, very exactly fitted. At the corner where the labyrinth ends there is, nearby, a pyramid two hundred and forty feet high.

In the Roman era, the Labyrinth was used as a stone quarry and thus destroyed; what little was left of its foundations was reused at the end of the nineteenth century in the construction of the Faiyum railroad line. The only excavations ever conducted were done by W.M.F. Petrie in 1889 and 1911, and he was able to find only a little of the original substance of the construction, including two large, entirely preserved granite shrines that sheltered statues of the king, along with some dozens of fragments of the monument's construction and statue programs. A possible explanation is that the classical description had nothing to do with the funerary temple of Amenemhet III, which, so far as we can tell, did not resemble what we read in Herodotus. It seems likely that Greek visitors to Hawara (perhaps not Herodotus himself) mistook the entire necropolis there including not only the temple but also hundreds of private tombs with their decorated superstructures and (inaccessible) subterranean burial chambers, where crocodile mummies (eventually found by Petrie) were laid to rest in the first millennium BCE (see **Question 45**), as the remains of a single, huge construction.

62.

Do we know any ancient Egyptian artists?

Egyptian art was mostly anonymous—in the end, it served not the artist, but the person who commissioned the work of art (see **Question 53**). And yet, a few artists are known to us, either through their own statements or through their expressive—and identifiable—handiwork, especially from the New Kingdom. During this period the artists who decorated the royal tombs in the Valley of the Kings decorated each other's tombs as well, which were mostly located along the cliff-face behind the artisan village of Deir el-Medina, on the west bank of Thebes (modern Luxor). By comparing the painting styles and specific details of, for example, the human figure, in private and royal tombs, we can sometimes identify the handiwork of particular artisans. This is particularly evident in the 18th Dynasty tomb of the "directors of painting in the Place of *Maat*" at Saqqara, which belonged to two master artists who decorated their own tomb, and whose hands are quite different. Perhaps the best attested artist of Egypt's New Kingdom is Tuthmosis, the court artist of Amarna, whose workshop—including the bust of Nefertiti and a number of lifelike gypsum masks—was found during the excavation of Akhetaten/Amarna.

In the text of a stela now in the Louvre, a Middle Kingdom artist named Irtisen left behind an extraordinary self-portrait. In it, Irtisen vaunts both his knowledge in preparing colors and the fact that there is no one but him and his son who distinguish themselves through such skill. Irtisen further boasts of the almost magical capability and creativity with which he captured the world in works of art:

> I am truly an artist who is versed in his art, who steps forth and stands at the fore through what he has learned. I know the grid [*i.e.*, the network of lines sketched on the surface prior to creating the drawings], the balancing of the canon of proportions [*i.e.*, for rendering human figures], sunk and raised relief, when it [*i.e.*, the relief] protrudes and sinks, so that the body comes to its [correct] place. I know the going of a man's form and the coming of a woman's figure, the pose of birds and cattle, the resignation of an individual captive, when one eye sees the other; [how] to make the face of enemies look fearful; the raising of the arm of one who harpoons a hippopotamus, the gait of one who is running.

 **63.**

What symbolism is found in the architecture of the royal tombs in the Valley of the Kings?

Until the beginning of Dynasty 18—that is, for a good 1,200 years—the pyramid was the basic form of Egyptian royal tombs. In the New Kingdom, however, the earliest royal tombs at Thebes were a combination of built and rock-cut structures on the cliffside and crowned with extremely modest pyramids that scarcely conformed to the ideal of the old tradition. With Thutmose I, a change in the concept of the royal afterlife became manifested in the construction and decoration of the royal tombs. The royal burial places were no longer visible from the Nile valley, but rather located in a wadi cut off from it by a barrier of rock—the Valley of the Kings—and took the form of tombs that extended deep into the earth. These tombs were no longer intended to assist in the royal ascent to the sky (see also **Question 55** with the discussion of Djoser's complex), but rather to begin the passage of the king's descent into the netherworld. From this point on the royal tombs of Dynasty 18 had an entrance in the north and continued, via four successive stairways and corridors, all the way to a shaft that might have symbolized the entrance to the subterranean caverns of the funerary god Sokar, whose realm is described in the fourth and fifth hours of the Amduat, one of the Books of the Netherworld (see also **Question 44**). With the antechamber that followed the shaft, the axis of the tomb shifted toward the east. The bent axis (like that in the pyramids of Dynasty 12) and the alternation of staircases and corridors represented the twisted paths of the netherworld, into which the tomb itself led. The oval shape of the sarcophagus chamber in the earlier tombs (with four side chambers) corresponded to the last hour of the night in the Amduat, out of which the newly reborn sun god emerged each morning (see also **Question 14**). This pathway into the netherworld is even more impressively realized in the tomb of Hatshepsut, which spirals 213 meters down into the depths; the sarcophagus chamber is 97 meters below the level of the entrance. Under Amenhotep II, the (now rectangular) sarcophagus chamber developed into two levels: a higher pillared hall and a sunken crypt containing the sarcophagus of the King. The tombs of this period also start to be more comprehensively decorated. Until the Amarna era, the burial chamber itself was reserved for the Amduat (whose more exact Egyptian title was *Book of the Hidden Chamber*), a guide to the netherworld that depicted the journey of the sun god through the realm beyond, including his regeneration, as well as his revivification and provisioning of the dead. From Dynasty 18 to Dynasty 20, each royal tomb contained innovations of some kind, whether in layout, decoration, or simply in the constantly increasing size of its corridors—a principle for which Erik Hornung has coined the term "extension of the existing."

The two largest and most complex tombs, both of them entirely decorated to a length of 100 meters, are that of Seti I, discovered in 1817 in an excellent state of preservation (but badly damaged by early excavators and then tourists), and that of his successor, Ramesses II (which was badly damaged by water already in antiquity). Each has about twenty different chambers, halls, passageways (originally closed off by doors), and corridors. Beyond the sarcophagus chamber of Seti I, which has an astronomical ceiling, a corridor leads into the depths for another 174 meters. The recent excavation of the tunnel by Zahi Hawass shows that the work was abandoned, probably when the King died, after only eight years of reign. A similar (as yet unexplored) tunnel seems to exist in the tomb of Ramesses II and may have been intended to reach the water table, which was conceived of by the Egyptians as part of the primeval ocean Nun, which surrounded the earth and remained the source of regeneration and rejuvenation. In Dynasty 19, a definitively new concept was realized under Merneptah, when the axis of the tomb was straightened. From Ramesses IV on, the tombs were nearly flat, no longer leading down steeply into the rock. Since a straight axis is attested for the first time in Akhenaten's royal tomb at Amarna, and since the entrance to the post-Amarna royal tombs in the Valley of the Kings was located mostly in the east or southeast, scholars have suspected that these innovations reflect the solar theology of Akhenaten, which necessitated that the sun be able to shine into the sarcophagus chamber and bring the King to life with its rays (see **Question 64**).

 **64.**

Was the art of the Amarna Period "naturalistic"?

At Amarna, the importance of nature was a direct conse-quence of Akhenaten's new theology, which no longer understood the world as the dwelling place of gods and goddesses whose effects needed to be explained by myths (see **Question 33**). At the center of this doctrine stood Aten, the sun in its physical manifestation. All statements about Aten were derived from empirical observations of the course of the sun, of its light and warmth, and of nature, which was created and kept alive by the sun. It was now possible to experience the divine in the open sun courts of the temple, in contrast to the traditional temples, where the cult image was hidden in the complete darkness of the holy of holies (see **Question 42**). Aten existed only as the physical sundisk in the sky, and he could not dwell in cult images, as was believed of the traditional deities. The text of the boundary stelae of the capital city of Amarna thus states: "who has built himself with his arms, sculptors do not know him." In traditional belief, closeness to divinity was supposed to be achieved through cult, but Aten, in his course through the sky, remained distant from the world. Images of nature itself now replaced myth, so that Akhenaten was no longer wished jubilee festivals as numerous "as those of the gods," but "as the grains of sand on the bank, as the scales of fish and the hairs of cattle, as the feathers of birds and the leaves of trees"!

Nature was, so to speak, the reflection of Aten's creative power, and it was thus the guideline for a new artistic style.

Instead of idealized depictions, there was now a more realistic and more individual rendering of persons, resulting in a new genre of portraiture that can be seen in the gypsum masks of Amarna, and in the emotions, movement, and emerging spatiality that now made their appearance in art. Along with this came new themes, such as the propagandistic representation of the royal family, idealized scenes of nature, and unusual scenes taken from everyday life (such as a servant sweeping a floor). A veritable "architecture of nature" made its appearance at Amarna, as we see most clearly in the southern temple complex of Maru-Aten, where a richly decorated, artificial, garden-like landscape evidently served the worship of Aten during the course of the year. In the "green room" of the North Palace there was an aviary, where the creation of birds could be observed and reproduced, such as was described, with unprecedented attention to detail, in the Great Hymn to the Aten. Even the adoption of Late Egyptian, the vernacular of the time, as the official literary language (see also **Question 69**) might have been a consequence of this realism. It is unlikely, however, that Akhenaten, by implementing his religion, anticipated one of the characteristic mottoes of the European Enlightenment, Jean-Jacques Rousseau's "back to nature," as Joachim Spiegel once suggested (1950). The naturalistic art of Amarna was not created for the sake of nature itself, but for the sake of Aten.

 **65.**

What influence did Egyptian art have on the classical world?

In the first millennium BCE and in the Roman era, Egyptian art was in vogue in the Near East and the Mediterranean world—from Phoenician anthropoid sarcophagi and the motifs carved on Phoenician ivories all the way to the architecture of Persia. For example, in the Apadana palace at Persepolis, Ionic column shafts have Egyptian palm capitals, and the door jambs were crowned with Egyptian cavetto cornices; we also see Egyptian sculptural ornamentation and inlay work. Darius I, who was also ruler of the satrapy of Egypt (see also **Question 94**), took so many Egyptian artists to Persia that we can clearly discern a decline in the quality of Egyptian art of the period. Egyptian motifs also figure in the stylish decoration of villas belonging to the Roman imperial family, such as the villa of Augustus' daughter Julia in Boscotrecase, or in the "House of Augustus" on the Palatine Hill in Rome.

While the Roman examples represent a form of fascination with Egypt, rather than stylistic influence in the strict sense of the term, precisely this type of influence has often been suggested for ancient Greek art, particularly in the case of statues of nude young men (*kouroi*) and of Archaic temples. Standing figures of nude youths appear, with no precursors, in Greek art of the Archaic period, around 600 BCE. They employ, though, the Egyptian canon of proportions (see also **Question 54**) in use during Dynasty 26 (the Saite Dynasty, *c.*685–525 BCE), and they display Egyptian "know-how" in the technique with which the stone is worked. Scholars have been more cautious in the matter of the origin of the Archaic Greek temple. The Classical Greek peripteral temple, with the building surrounded by a colonnade, can be traced back to precursors in Greece itself, though such temples are also attested in Egypt. The first stone peripteral temples are attested at eighth-century Ephesus, and at Corinth (temple of Isthmia) in the first half of the seventh century; in these cases, a communication of Egyptian ideas via Phoenicians seems conceivable. Especially striking, and probably inspired by Egypt, is the newly conceived monumental temple of Hera on Samos built in 530 BCE. Originally constructed in 575 BCE, the second incarnation was 100 times larger in volume than the original building. The architects used the Egyptian cubit as their unit of measurement, and they employed Egyptian construction techniques, such as a sand foundation bed, for the second temple. Ever since the seventh century, the elites of Egypt and the Greek world had enjoyed a very close relationship. Pharaoh Amasis (570–526 BCE), who ruled at the time of the monumental construction on Samos, was married to a Greek woman from Cyrene. He granted commercial privileges to the Greek trading settlement of Naukratis in the Nile Delta, concluded treaties with Lydia, Samos, and Cyrene, and contributed votive offerings to the temples of Cyrene, Rhodes, and Samos. These political relations between Egypt and Samos provide a specific historical context for the proposed transfer of architectural knowledge.

66.

To whom does ancient Egyptian art belong?

Today, there is a lively discussion regarding the conservation and ownership of Egyptian art. What steps can be taken to prevent the looting of archaeological sites in contemporary Egypt, an activity stimulated by the demands of the western art market and dramatically furthered by the lack of security following the Egyptian revolution in 2011? And can Egypt insist on the return of art objects legally, if not in hindsight always ethically, acquired by western nations during the nineteenth and early twentieth centuries? The great western collections of Egyptian art—those in the Metropolitan Museum in New York, British Museum in London, the Louvre in Paris, the Egyptian Museum in Berlin, and the Egyptian Museum in Turin—owe their huge holdings of tens of thousands of objects to a far-flung policy of imperialistic enrichment during the nineteenth and twentieth centuries. Still, we must note that this policy led to the preservation of art works that would otherwise probably have been lost or destroyed. From 1882 to 1922, Egypt was under British administration, and it was then more or less a British protectorate until the establishment of the Republic in 1953. Until 1952, the Egyptian Antiquities Service remained in French hands. In any event, the fact that the discovery of the tomb of Tutankhamun in 1922 coincided with the formal independence of Egypt meant that the entire tomb treasure remained the property of Egypt. Egypt could also now impose stronger regulations on the export of antiquities, hire Egyptian staff for the Antiquities Service, and train native Egyptologists, as called for in 1923 by Egypt's first Egyptologist, Ahmad

Kamal. With Egypt's full independence, Mustafa Amer became the first Egyptian director of the Antiquities Service. The UNESCO campaign to save the antiquities of Nubia (see also **Question 67**), started in 1960, resulted in a trailblazing international cooperation. In return for the international help it received, Egypt donated monuments (such as the temple of Dendur to the Metropolitan Museum of Art), authorized traveling exhibitions (especially the Tutankhamun exhibitions), and granted excavation permits.

Today, Egypt partners with many foreign institutions that significantly contribute personnel, finances, and technical expertise to the excavation and preservation of Egypt's pharaonic, Christian, and Islamic past. There are international agreements intended to prevent the flourishing trade in antiquities from Egypt, a trade that is driven by western interest in Egyptian art and contributes to the destruction of monuments in Egypt. A return of the great foreign collections of Egyptian art to the Arab Republic of Egypt, in as far as they were removed from the country as a consequence of the imperialistic policies of the past, is today neither politically likely nor practicable—space and funding to exhibit and scientifically manage them are not available. But the Egyptian economy stands to gain through increased tourism from the presence of Egyptian works of art in western countries, where there is markedly more interest in ancient Egypt than there is in Egypt itself (see **Question 8**). Nevertheless, it seems both necessary and feasible to make compromises, ranging from the return or exchange of certain art works, to the conversion of legal ownership into a permanent loan status.

67.

What modern text invites us to reflect on Egyptian art?

At the time when UNESCO made its appeal to save the antiquities of Nubia, which were threatened by the construction of the High Dam at Aswan, the French writer André Malraux composed the third of his "Funeral Orations," the text "To Save the Monuments of Upper Egypt," dated March 8, 1960. An extract from this lengthy text is given here without comment, so as not to detract from its effect (translation by Francis Joseph Preston, with some minor modifications):

> With our century has arisen one of the greatest events of the history of the mind. These temples which one had only seen as vestiges, have again become monuments; these statues have found a soul. Refound their own? Certainly not. A soul which belongs to them, that is found only in them, but one which no one has found there before us.
>
> We speak of this art as the testament of a civilization in the same way that we speak of Romanesque art as being a testimony of Roman Christianity. Yet we really know only surviving civilizations. Despite the work of Egyptologists, the faith of a priest of Amun, the fundamental attitude of an Egyptian regarding the world, remain unreachable. The humour of the ostraka, the little people of the figurines, the text where a soldier of Ramses II calls him by his nickname, Rara,

like the old guard called Napoleon, the ironic wisdom of the juridical texts, how do you connect these to the *Book of the Dead*, to the funereal majesty of the great effigies, to a civilization which seems only to have been pursued for three thousand years because of its otherworld. The only living ancient Egypt for us is that suggested by Egyptian art—and this Egypt has never existed. No more than the Christianity suggested to us by Romanesque art, were it the sole testimony. The survival of Egypt is in its art and not in illustrious names or lists of victories ... despite Kadesh, perhaps one of the most decisive battles of history, despite the cartouches chiselled out and reinscribed on the order of the Pharaoh that attempted to impose his posteriority on the gods; Sesostris is less present for us than poor Akhenaton. And the face of the queen Nefertiti haunts our artists as that of Cleopatra haunts our poets. But Cleopatra was a queen without a face, and Nefertiti is a face without a queen.

Egypt survives, therefore, by a domain of forms. And we know today that these forms, like those of all civilizations of the sacred, are defined by their reference to the living, whom they seem to imitate, but by a style which gives them access to a world that is not that of the living. The Egyptian style is elaborated to make of these highest forms the mediators between ephemeral men and the constellations which direct them. It has deified the night. It is this which we all feel when we approach the front of the sphinx of Giza, this which I felt the last time I saw it at nightfall: 'In the distance the second pyramid closes the perspective and makes of the colossal funeral mask, the guardian of a trap directed against the waves of the desert and against the shadows. It is the hour when the oldest governed forms rediscover that silken rustling by which the desert answers the immemorial prostration of the Orient; the hours when they animate the place where the gods spoke, chase the formless immensity, and order the constellations which seem to issue from the night only to gravitate around them.'

And so the Egyptian style, for three thousand years, has translated the perishable into the eternal.

Understand well that it does not touch us solely as a testimony of history, or as what until not long ago was called beauty. Beauty has become one of the foremost enigmas of our time, the mysterious presence by which the works of Egypt are united to the statues of our cathedrals and the Aztec temples, to those of the caves of India and of China—to the pictures of Cézanne and Van Gogh, to those of the greatest living artists and greatest dead—in the Treasure of the first world civilization.

A gigantic resurrection, of which the Renaissance will soon appear to us as only a timid rough draft. For the first time humanity has discovered a universal language of art. We feel clearly its power, even if we know poorly its nature. Without a doubt this power comes from the fact that this treasure of art, of which humanity is taking cognizance for the first time, brings to us the resounding victory of human works over death. To the invincible 'never again' which reigns over history, this surviving Treasure opposes its solemn enigma. Of the power that made Egypt surge out of the prehistoric night, nothing remains; but the power which made these now-threatened colossi, and the masterpieces of the Cairo museum, speaks to us with a voice as loud as that of the masters of Chartres, as that of Rembrandt. With the authors of these granite statues, we do not even have in common the same sentiment of love, or that of death— or even perhaps a similar way of regarding their works; but before these works, the imprint of the anonymous sculptors, forgotten for two millennia, seems to us as invulnerable to the succession of empires as the imprint of maternal love.

6

Egyptian Language and Literature

68.

Is ancient Egyptian still spoken today and are there any traces of ancient Egyptian in our modern languages?

Following the conquest of Egypt by Alexander the Great in 332 BCE, Greek became the official language of the administration and the elite. Egyptian remained the language of the provinces and the native population, though bilingualism was also common. Even so, the Demotic language and script remained as common for administrative and literary texts as the monumental hieroglyphic writing system for the great Graeco-Roman temples of Dendara, Edfu, Kom Ombo, Esna, and Philae. The decisive factor in the long-term demise of the native scripts and language was the rise of the monotheistic religions: Christianity and then Islam. With the triumph of Christianity, a variant of the Greek alphabet with the addition of a few signs taken from Demotic was introduced for the purpose of rendering Christian texts into the contemporary stage of the Egyptian language. The resultant script and language, which we call Coptic (Christian Egyptians are called "Copts"; see **Question 70**), became the dominant form, while the Demotic language and script fell out of use. This change of writing systems proved to be both a brilliant innovation and a catastrophe for the survival of the traditional culture. The abandonment of the old writing system also meant the loss of any access to the written culture of pharaonic Egypt—the last preserved document written in Demotic is a stela set up in honor of the sacred Buchis bull in the year 452 CE. Nonetheless, at the time of the Arab conquest of Egypt in 641 CE, about one-third of the population still adhered to the traditional religion, while the rest were Copts. After the Arab conquest of Egypt, Coptic, as the spoken Egyptian language, fell victim to the spread of Islam and the use of Arabic. Arabic was decreed to be the sole administrative language. The Fatimid caliph al-Hakim bi-amr Illah (996–1020 CE) forbade the speaking of Coptic, both in public and in private. High taxes on Coptic monasteries led to their decline as custodians of Coptic language and literature, resulting in a decreasing mastery of Coptic and the introduction of Arabic as the language of church services. In the middle of the fourteenth century, an Upper Egyptian monk glorified the doomed Coptic tongue in a didactic poem, the "Triadon." In the fifteenth century, the historian al-Maqrizi reported that Coptic was still spoken in Upper Egypt and at Assiut in Middle Egypt, though only by women and children. Purported last speakers of Coptic were occasionally mentioned in the seventeenth century. Around 1870, an old Copt at Qus stated for the official record that when he was a small boy, he heard his parents speaking Coptic with one another. A Coptic tradition in a place called Zinniyah was reported in the early twentieth century, but scholars have disputed the matter.

Since the early 1960s, there have been attempts to resuscitate Coptic (in its Bohairic dialect; see **Question 70**) as a spoken language in Coptic families, and Coptic is used in a few monasteries as the everyday language of the monks. There have been some textbooks of modern Coptic, complete with terms coined for modern innovations, such as "refrigerator" and "airplane." But Coptic, in its Bohairic dialect, is above all the language of church liturgy, much like Latin used to be in the Catholic Church. It has also exercised an enduring influence on the vocabulary and syntax of modern Egyptian Arabic. But it would be misleading to think in terms of any official promotion or revival of Coptic, for Islam is the official religion of Egypt, and Coptic Christianity, though theoretically recognized as equal, is in practice the object of discrimination and repression. In today's English, a number of probably

Egyptian words are still being used—such as adobe, alabaster, alum(inium), ammonia, barque, basalt, chemistry, ebony, gum, ibis, natron and natrium, oasis, and even in personal names such as Susanna ("lotus").

 **69.**

Could Queens Hetepheres, Nefertiti, and Cleopatra have had a chat?

Roughly 1,300 years of historical and linguistic development separated Queen Hetepheres (the presumed mother of Khufu, *c.*2600 BCE) from Queen Nefertiti (*c.*1350), and the same is true of Nefertiti and Cleopatra (Cleopatra VII, 51–30 BCE). Had they ever been able to get together, would they have been able to talk to each other? This is a more difficult question than we might expect, for from the Middle Kingdom (*c.*2000 BCE) on, different stages of the Egyptian spoken and written language were in use concurrently (see **Question 70**). From the Middle Kingdom through Dynasty 18, texts were composed in Middle Egyptian, but citations of direct speech, intrusions of the spoken language into the written, and other explicit indications show that during this period the spoken language was in the process of deviating from the written language. For example, officials were exhorted to be "free of saying *pa*"— that is, they were urged not to use the definite article *pa* ("the") from the spoken language, for there was no definite article in Middle Egyptian, which remained the standard language for official communication. Scholars suspect that until the Amarna Period, Egypt offered a case of diglossia, somewhat like the German-speaking part of Switzerland or the Arab countries today, where two variants of the same language are used side by side, one of them serving as the literary language and the other as the vernacular. Under Akhenaten (see also **Question**

33), the spoken vernacular of Late Egyptian (as we call it today) was decreed to be the literary language, thus bringing an end to the state of diglossia. And yet, classical Middle Egyptian continued to be used as the language of historical and religious texts down into the Roman era, and as a learned language, it was still read and recited, a situation comparable to the use of Latin in the Middle Ages and the early modern period.

The Old Egyptian preserved in texts, the language of the period of Hetepheres, the presumed wife of Snofru and mother of Khufu, was an early stage of classical Middle Egyptian. Thus, the language actually spoken by the queen, probably a somewhat progressive vernacular, might have been rather like what we know as Middle Egyptian. The traditional high standard language of Dynasty 18 (Middle Egyptian), which Nefertiti surely mastered along with the Late Egyptian variant, would certainly have sounded somewhat different from the language of the Old Kingdom. Even so, it would have been possible for her to communicate with Hetepheres, at least by writing in hieroglyphs (although not in Hieratic, the cursive handwriting, which would have differed too much!). Late Egyptian, however, whether written or spoken, would have been largely incomprehensible to Hetepheres, for it had not only a partially different vocabulary, but also a linguistic structure and grammar that differed from Middle Egyptian. As an example, in the earlier stage of the language, we find "synthetic" verb forms, similar to "they sang," while later, the past tense was expressed with the use of an auxiliary verb: "they did sing." Such "analytic" constructions are characteristic for the later stage—for instance, a future form similar to English "I am going to do" or French "je vais faire." In Old Egyptian, the possessive pronoun always followed the noun, and the noun never had an article: thus, "father our" for "our father." In the later stages of the language, however, the pronoun was attached to the article and both preceded the noun: "the our father." There were also new pronouns unknown to Old Egyptian, as well as new sentence structures.

And what about communication between Nefertiti and Cleopatra? Cleopatra was the first (and only) Ptolemaic ruler competent in ancient Egyptian, which in her day was Demotic. The Late Egyptian spoken by Nefertiti, like the Demotic spoken by Cleopatra, belonged to the later version of the Egyptian language. But Demotic vocabulary and grammar had evolved beyond Late Egyptian, so that Nefertiti would have had a more difficult job understanding Cleopatra than the latter would have had understanding Nefertiti. Nonetheless, the two could have resorted to written communication using Middle Egyptian, provided that Cleopatra refrained from indulging in the spellings of the Ptolemaic inscriptions which would have been confusing for Nefertiti. Communication among the three queens would thus perhaps have been possible using Middle Egyptian—if not out loud, then in writing, at least, and if they used hieroglyphs rather than the cursive scripts for everyday use (*i.e.*, hieratic and Demotic).

70.

How many languages were spoken in ancient Egypt?

At any given time, different dialects of one and the same stage of the Egyptian language—and, to a certain extent, different stages of the language (see **Question 69**)—were spoken along the Nile, along with a considerable number of foreign languages. We have knowledge of the dialects almost exclusively from Coptic, the final stage of the Egyptian language, which was written with the Greek alphabet and a few additional letters, including vowels, which were not indicated in the earlier phases of the language. For Coptic, which was spoken from the first century CE to the early modern period (see **Question 68**), scholars distinguish at least seven principal dialects: Sahidic ("Upper Egyptian," though it was originally the dialect of Memphis), Bohairic ("Lower Egyptian"), Faiyumic in the western oasis of the Faiyum, Mesokemic in the mid-Nile valley, and, in the regions of the respective cities, Hermopolitan (around Hermopolis), Lykopolitan (around Lykopolis), and Akhmimic (around Akhmim). Like the various Arabic dialects spoken in Egypt today, these Coptic dialects were pronounced differently, and there were also differences in their vocabulary and grammar. From among these dialects, Sahidic and Bohairic became the literary languages of the Coptic Church. At present, other dialects are attested only in a few manuscripts, or their very existence has been questioned, as in the case of "Bashmuric," a dialect described as extinct by the grammarian Athanasius of Qus in the fourteenth century.

In the border areas of Egypt, various other languages were spoken: speakers of Semitic languages were settled between the northeastern Delta and the land bridge to Palestine, while the western Delta was a transitional area into the region where Libyan (an early form of modern Berber) was spoken. Similarly, the linguistic border with the Libyan-Berber region ran along the high desert plateau west of the Nile valley—in Egypt's Siwa oasis, a Berber dialect is spoken to this very day. Kushitic languages, a large phylum of the Afroasiatic languages in Northeast Africa, must have been spoken in the southeast of Egypt; in modern times, the linguistic border with Bedja/Bisharin (a North Kushitic language) has been located at the latitude of Luxor. In addition, ancient Egypt's Nubian border at the First Cataract remains the habitat of Nubian population groups. Finally, in all periods, many speakers of foreign languages came to live in Egypt as a result of immigration and trade, or as prisoners of war (see also **Questions 32 and 50**); in the capital cities of the second and first millennia, there were even ethnic neighborhoods. During the two periods of Persian rule (between the late sixth and the late fourth centuries BCE), Imperial Aramaic was the administrative language of the Egyptian province (satrapy) of the Persian Empire. From the seventh century BCE on, the era when Demotic was spoken, an increasing number of Greeks settled in Egypt, and in Ptolemaic and Roman times, Greek was the language of the Hellenistic elite and the royal administration (see also **Question 68**).

 # 71.

Who could read hieroglyphs in ancient Egypt?

In all periods of Egyptian history, literacy was a privilege, an instrument of the elite, distinguishing them from the rest of the population and defining their status. The literate were always a small percentage of the population: according to a recent estimate, only a third of one percent to, at most, one percent. In the Old Kingdom, this would have been about 5,000–15,000 (which seems too large) out of an estimated population of 1 to 1.5 million. In the Late Period, out of a population of perhaps 4–5 million, it would have been at most 50,000 persons. We must also take into account varying degrees of mastery of the writing system: people who could only read versus those who could both read and write, and whether they were literate in the cursive scripts of administration (Demotic, Hieratic: Figure 13), or also in the hieroglyphic version used for monumental inscriptions.

During the later fourth millennium BCE, when writing made its first appearance in Egypt, the number of individuals expert in the new communication system must have been even more limited. There is reason to believe that the idea of writing was introduced to Egypt from Mesopotamia, prompting the development of a genuine Egyptian script after 3500 BCE. Until the late 1980s, the earliest writing preserved to us occurred on cylinder seals, palettes, pottery vessels, and labels from the period after 3000 BCE, when the writing system was already fully developed. The situation changed in 1988, when royal tomb U-j in the Predynastic cemetery at Abydos yielded the (so far) earliest known writing, dating to around 3200 BCE, and thus pushing the horizon of the appearance of the writing system back by at least 200 years. These inscriptions on jars and labels consisted of only one to four signs each, and they presumably indicated either the contents of the jars and containers, or the contents' place of origin. Strikingly, the same period also yielded other systems of notation that have yet to be deciphered: so-called pot marks (scratch marks on vessels), petroglyphs from the end of the fourth millennium, and otherwise unknown hieroglyphs on Predynastic seal impressions from Abydos. In Egypt, we still have no precursors to the writing system now attested from about 3200 BCE on, but for Mesopotamia, scholars have proposed a derivation of writing from an attested system of conveying information—indications of numbers on "tokens" made of clay—that dates back to about 8000 BCE. From this much longer prehistory of written communication in Uruk (or Elam), along with the otherwise strong cultural influence of Mesopotamia on Egypt (see **Question 57**), it seems plausible that the idea of writing came from Mesopotamia. However, it is clear that the ancient Egyptians created from this a distinct system suited to Egyptian needs.

In the Roman era, starting in the second century CE, the mandatory use of Greek for the province's administration and the spread of Christianity led to a dramatic decline in the knowledge of the Egyptian writing system. The rise of Egyptian Christianity required the translation of Christian texts, at first especially the Old and New Testaments, into the native language, Coptic (that is, the last stage of the ancient Egyptian language). For that reason, the last expression of the genuinely Egyptian writing system, called Demotic, was essentially given up (though it continued to be used by non-Christian Egyptians), and the Greek alphabet was adopted, along with a few additional letters taken from Demotic (see **Questions 68** and **70**). Earlier attempts to write Egyptian with Greek letters plus additional signs not used in Greek are attested as early as the third century BCE, in particular, for magical texts that absolutely had to be pronounced

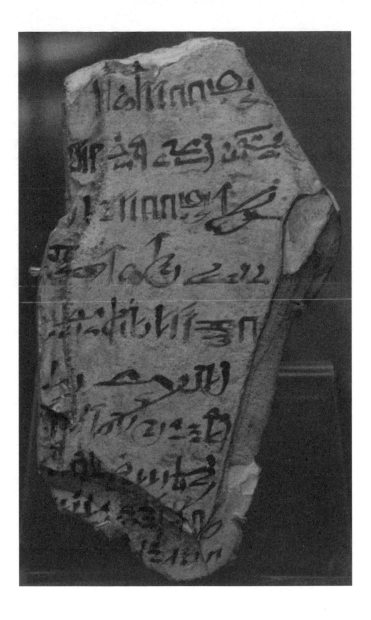

Figure 13: A limestone flake from the Valley of the Kings on which the names of officials who were involved in the inspection of tombs are recorded in Hieratic script. Dynasty 21

correctly. Some so-called "Old Coptic" (especially magical and astrological) texts are earlier than or contemporary with the rise of actual Coptic, which we find from the end of the second century CE on.

At this time, Greek was the language of the elites, including Egypt's Christian theologians who were active at Alexandria (*e.g.*, Clement, Origen, Didymus, Athanasius, Cyril), while Egyptian was the language of the provinces and the native population, though many people were bilingual. Knowledge of the ancient, traditional writing systems dwindled over time, until it was confined to the priests of the pagan temples, the very last of which was the temple of Philae. The last hieroglyphic text comes from the year 394 CE, and the last Demotic inscription from 452 CE.

 **72.**

Did the Egyptians have a cryptic writing system?

In the broader sense of the term, the Egyptian writing system was always cryptic, because it was accessible only to a small proportion of the population (see **Question 71**). In the narrower sense, coded writing (so-called cryptography) is attested from as early as the Old Kingdom, and was particularly prominent in the Graeco-Roman Period; it was used mainly in religious texts. It operated using the distinctive nature of the hieroglyphic writing system itself, which principally employed phonetic signs, but also made use of signs that retained their pictographic character (see also **Question 79**). For example, the simple expression *amaf* "in it" was written with the three phonetic signs *i–m–f*, which were also a sequence of images: *reed leaf–owl–horned viper*. In cryptography, such sign sequences could be used to encode a second, hidden message along with the actual phonetic sequence. This was achieved by assigning the hieroglyphs different phonetic values, a process that followed a small number of rules. For example, similar signs (such as pictures of birds) could substitute for one another, or certain signs could receive new phonetic values according to the first sound in the word represented by the sign (the principle of "acrophony"). Thus, a frequently attested cryptographic writing of the divine name Amun (pronounced *Amanu* in the New Kingdom) uses the hieroglyph depicting an island (a long oval), with the hieroglyph depicting a ripple of water inserted inside it. Pictographically, this writing is to be read as "island with '*n*' (the phonetic value of the water hieroglyph)," which in Egyptian is *a-ma-n*.

In certain cases, a cryptographic text is executed as a three-dimensional sculpture or two-dimensional relief, thus disguising the fact that the image is also a text that can be read. For instance, the representation in relief of a funerary procession on a First Intermediate Period stela now in the Louvre can be read, figure after figure, as a cryptographic inscription, as is also the case with the frieze of baboons above the entrance to the temple of Ramesses II at Abu Simbel (see also **Question 45**). Sometimes normal hieroglyphic texts contain sections written in a wholly cryptographic manner, such as the cryptographic chapter 33 of the "Book of Gates" or certain hymns to the gods Khnum and Sobek in the temple of Esna. In the latter case long rows of rams or crocodiles are used within the text of the hymn, with only minute changes in the animals' appearance—for example, the addition of a crown, indicating to the knowledgeable the correct readings.

If a deeper, hidden meaning lay behind certain signs, the real-world persons or objects underlying the signs could then right away be understood as divine writing transplanted into the world. Returning to the example given just above, an actual island with water could have been conceived as a place where the god Amun was manifestly present. The "linguistic philosophy" lying behind this cryptography found a sort of continuation much later, in the early modern period, when scholars imagined that hieroglyphic inscriptions constituted an encoded knowledge of the cosmos that would be accessible to those initiated in how to decode it (see Preface).

# 73.

How did the ancient Egyptians do multiplication and division?

Like us, the ancient Egyptians had a decimal system with specific numerical signs for 1, 10, 100, 1,000, 10,000, 100,000, and 1,000,000. But in contrast to our notation, in which each numeral indicates a power of 10 by its position in the number (for instance, 4567 = 4 thousand 5 hundred, *etc.*), the Egyptians juxtaposed the individual number of numerals in groups: ꜥꜥꜥꜥꜥ∩∩IIIII = 536. Moreover, they had no special sign for "0."

Multiplication was done in a roundabout manner by doubling the multiplicand (see Figure 1). In a problem like 27 X 36, the multiplicand (36) was doubled in a series of steps: 36, 72, 144, *etc.* As it was doubled, the steps were noted in a parallel column as 1, 2, 4, *etc.* (*i.e.*, the sequence of powers of 2). In contemporary terminology, this process corresponds to a binary partitioning of the multiplier (27). They knew that the right number of steps was achieved as soon as the powers of two, added together, yielded the multiplier (27): 27 = 16 + 8 + 2 + 1 ($2^4 + 2^3 + 2^1 + 2^0$); because 2^2, which is 4, does not allow for the multiplicand to be obtained, it is left out of the equation. Thus, the desired final product is the sum of the corresponding doublings—that is, 36 ($2^0 = 1$ X 36) + 72 ($2^1 = 2$ X 36) + 288 ($2^3 = 8$ X 36) + 576 ($2^4 = 16$ X 36) = 972.

Division was done analogously, using the same listing of multiples, and the process can be illustrated using the same example: 972 (dividend) ÷ 36 (divisor) = ? (value of the quotient; see Figure 2). The column containing the steps of the doubling (powers of 2) broke off when the next step would exceed the dividend (in this case, 972)—that is, with 576. Then all the powers of 2 were added up whose corresponding doubled values, added together, equaled, or were less than, 972 (16 + 8 + 2 + 1 = 27). In this case, the division works out. If there was a remainder, it was expressed as a fraction of the divisor (See Figure 3). In our example, if the dividend had been 1,000 instead of 972, there would have been a remainder of 28, thus $^{28}/_{36}$ = $^{7}/_{9}$. There was a problem, however, in that ancient Egyptian mathematics knew only unit fractions (fractions with 1 as the numerator: $^{1}/_{2}$, $^{1}/_{4}$, *etc.*), along with a few complement fractions, such as $^{2}/_{3}$ and $^{3}/_{4}$. To calculate the fraction, the Egyptians continued the doubling steps in reverse order, thus listing each successive half value of 36: 18 (= $^{1}/_{2}$ of 36), 9 (= $^{1}/_{4}$ of 36). At this point, the Egyptians had reached 18 + 9 = 27 (leaving 28—27 = 1 as the numerator of the last fraction, a unit fraction), so that the result of 1000 ÷ 36 was 27 + $^{1}/_{2}$ + $^{1}/_{4}$ + $^{1}/_{36}$.

1. Problem: 27 x 36 = **972**

added doublings

$2^0 = 1$	36
$2^1 = 2$	72
$2^2 = 4$	144
$2^3 = 8$	288
$2^4 = 16$ 1 + 2 + 8 + 16 = 27	576 36 + 72 + 288 + 576 = **972**

2. Problem: $972 \div 36 = 27$
doublings in reverse order

1152	
576 $36 + 72 + 288 + 576 = 972$	$2^4 = 16$ $1 + 2 + 8 + 16 = 27$
288	$2^3 = 8$
144	$2^2 = 4$
72	$2^1 = 2$
36	$2^0 = 1$

3. Problem: $1000 \div 36 - 27 \rightarrow$ **remainder** $28 = {}^{28}/_{36} = {}^{7}/_{9}$

$18 = {}^{1}/_{2}$ of 36	
$9 = {}^{1}/_{4}$ of 36	
remainder $1 = {}^{1}/_{36}$	

$1000 \div 36 = 27 + {}^{1}/_{2} + {}^{1}/_{4} + {}^{1}/_{36}$

74.

What do we mean by "Egyptian Literature"?

Until the 1970s, Egyptologists made rather intuitive decisions as to what should be regarded as literature or "fine literature." Since then, however, there has been intensive discussion of this problem. For the most part, scholars have come to a narrower definition than the previous, extremely liberal characterization of literature as everything that was not intended to document legal proceedings or a text intended for technical use. In the earlier view, literature was to be contrasted, in particular, to written documents and records that laid no claim to artistic or aesthetic merit. But this distinction is not always so easy to make. Among ancient Egyptian writings there was indeed utilitarian literature with aesthetic claims, from funerary literature to handbooks, while there were also texts scholars have traditionally qualified as literary that were used in a professional context, such as the "instruction" texts written for the education of future government bureaucrats.

The two principal recent proposals to define ancient Egyptian literature have been made by Jan Assmann and Antonio Loprieno. The former bases his definition on the use of texts, and thus on external factors, while the latter looks to internal textual criteria. Assmann makes a basic, threefold categorization of the texts that have survived to us from ancient Egypt, distinguishing "literature" from "archives" and "monuments." In his view, literature can be subdivided into *literature of knowledge*, *literature of education*, *entertainment literature* (though it is highly dubious that there was any literature intended solely to entertain), and *literature of recitation.* He considers literature of knowledge to be "texts regarded by us as 'literary' or 'belles lettres'," and which "were clearly viewed by the ancient Egyptians as cultural texts—that is, educative texts that a culture sees as expressing a valid formulation of its world view." In practice, however, this classification runs into a number of problems, since many texts that were viewed as "literary" did anything but belong to the category of literature of knowledge—texts from love poetry to Late Egyptian tales (see also **Question 34**). They were even recorded on monuments, such as the poem describing the Battle of Kadesh or the literary account on the Piankhy Stela (and would thus not belong to literature altogether). By way of contrast, Loprieno's more normative, narrower concept qualifies as literature only that which displays "select characteristics of literarity." These characteristics are, in particular: fictionality (without any unambiguous references to reality), intertextuality (references to other texts belonging to a literary universe), and later reception (though this is often not demonstrable in ancient Egypt because of the hazards of preservation). Other criteria of literature, though they are somewhat problematic for Egypt, are literary freedom and autonomy (literature is independent of constraints prevalent in other forms of expression, and it contains ambiguity), self-reference (literary statements always refer back to themselves), the transmission of norms that are concretized by their being adopted (poiesis/mimesis), and the aesthetic quality of texts. The study of literature is thus one of the few areas of Egyptology in which academic debates in the primary discipline (in this case, literary studies) have been taken note of and adopted. This is a step forward, though it also requires awareness of what methods of literary interpretation would not be suitable for the evidence from Egypt.

75.

Who wrote ancient Egyptian literature, and for whom was it written?

A papyrus of the New Kingdom—Papyrus Chester-Beatty IV—stresses the enduring importance of literary works, while monuments of stone fall into ruin. In this connection, it gives a catalogue of past authors:

> Is there one here like Hardedef? Is there another like Imhotep? None of our kin is like Neferti, or Khety, the foremost among them. I give you the name of Ptahemdjehuty, of Khakheperresonb. Is there another like Ptahhotep, or the equal of Kaires?

These were well-known elite officials of the Old and Middle Kingdoms whose individual reputations evidently led to their being identified as major figures in literary and cultural tradition—even though, so far as we know, not one of them actually authored works of literature. As in the case of works of art (see **Question 62**), the authors of Egyptian texts are mostly anonymous to us, with only a few exceptions, such as the author of a New Kingdom instructional text, Amunnakht, who is attested as one of the scribes in the workmen's settlement of Deir el-Medina in the west of Thebes, or King Akhenaten as the supposed author of the Great Hymn to the Aten at Amarna.

We know equally little about the performance, recitation, or readership of literary texts. Certain textual genres probably had a specific place in real life—the instructional texts in the education of state officials, biographical inscriptions in the tombs of private individuals, historical stelae in the legitimation of political actions in the context of temples (see also **Question 76**). There is, however, much disagreement as to the historical contextualizing and significance of the numerous Middle and Late Egyptian stories. These tales, which mostly concern the royal court and kingship, include such Middle Egyptian examples as the Tale of the Shipwrecked Sailor, the Story of Sinuhe, the Complaints of the Eloquent Peasant (see **Question 39**), the tales of wonder in Papyrus Westcar, and a text regarding the athletic achievements of Amenemhet II in the Faiyum. It seems thus possible to speak of many of these texts as a sort of court literature whose authors were part of the royal residence and came from among the state elite.

A broad range of modern approaches has been employed to interpret and classify works such as these. Some scholars view these texts as aesthetic works of art, irrespective of their genuine historical context. Others see them as entertainment literature or, quite to the contrary, as instruments of contemporary religious and political ideology. Also problematic is the fact that in many cases we cannot determine when the texts were initially composed because only later copies of the original work exist and the Middle or Late Egyptian literary language employed does not provide us with any clues. Thus, the extent to which they reflect real political situations or should be seen as a commentary on contemporary issues, or perhaps some combination thereof (with or without entertainment value), remains uncertain.

76.

Why do Egyptian historical texts describe nothing negative?

According to the official ideology, the king was the guarantor of world order; so long as he reigned, no harm could come to Egypt (see **Question 46**). An attack on Egypt or political opposition to the king was thus described as a rebellion against the order of *creation* (*i.e.*, *Maat*; see **Question 39**), and had to be put down by the king. For magical reasons alone, such an incursion of the world of chaos could not be set down in writing, for doing so would lend reality and duration to the destruction of order (see **Question 40**). With few exceptions, we learn of the reality of Egyptian life only from written administrative documents whose survival was not anticipated.

In the realm of royalty, we hardly ever encounter retrospective reports containing critical mention of political mistakes. There are some exceptions, such as the Instruction for King Merikare, the Instruction of King Amenemhet, and the historical section of the Great Papyrus Harris, in which these words are placed in the mouth of Ramesses III: "Listen so that I may tell you about my good deeds that I carried out when I was king for humankind." These texts were, however, composed to affirm the political legitimacy of these kings' successors on the throne, and thus have an underlying agenda that includes casting their predecessor in an unflattering manner. In some cases, reading between the lines can reveal what was deliberately left in silence. Thus a temporal gap of two weeks in the depiction of the Syrian expedition of Amenhotep II, after which he returned south indicates not only that he must have been in the north, but also betrays that he had evidently been beaten back while attempting an incursion into the territory of the kingdom of Mitanni. Since such an event contradicted the image required by royal ideology, it was left out of the formal account; only the dates transferred from the war diary onto a stela reveal the suppressed fact. For the most part, it was not until after the Ramesside Period that royal texts, sometimes, displayed a commitment to historical reality. Two noteworthy examples are when the Kushite King Piankhy, who conquered Egypt around 730 BCE, acknowledged the existence of other kings in Egypt, or when Amasis looked back on the struggle against his predecessor and legitimate king of Egypt, Apries.

The private autobiographies from the Old Kingdom onward are similar in portraying an ideal picture, and not a real account, of the life and career of the deceased. Although tomb inscriptions were explicitly intended to be read by both the deceased's contemporaries and future generations, they communicate for the most part only what was in accordance with *Maat* (see **Question 39**), and thus was worthy of being recorded. With few exceptions, we search in vain for failures, illnesses, and mistakes. Yet the existence of magical spells and rituals to ward them off indicates not only that unfortunate, even dire, things certainly occurred (see **Questions 40** and **51**), but also the degree to which the ancient Egyptians were concerned with them. An exceptional acknowledgment of a bad life is preserved in the heartfelt plea for funerary offerings made by the childless Padisobek, a priest of Neith from the Hellenistic period, who had spent a pitiful "life in sickness and pain from morning to night" and who says in his biography: "I am a tree with its roots ripped out because of what happened to me!"

77.

Were there comics in ancient Egypt?

In Egypt, pictures and words went hand in hand. The relationship between word and image covered the whole spectrum of possibilities: pictures with captions (adding names, titles, terms, or activities), texts with illustrations (such as the vignettes of the spells of the Book of the Dead), detailed versions in text and images that are relatively autonomous (such as the Books of the Netherworld), and "history paintings" accompanied by detailed texts (as in the case of Ramesses II's Battle of Kadesh). Actual precursors of modern comic strips—a narrative sequence of images, sometimes with explanatory captions or the words spoken by the people involved—are attested since the Old Kingdom. They first occur in the daily life scenes in private tombs, which could extend over several registers of a lively depiction of activities. The free spaces in the depictions are often filled in with encouraging shouts, humorous remarks, swear words, songs, and dialogues. The major New Kingdom Books of the Netherworld are composed in the form of twelve "illustrated broadsheets" (one for each hour of the night), each divided into three horizontal registers. The middle register is reserved for the journey of the sun god Re, and we are to imagine that the upper and lower registers represent the riverbanks on either side of his nocturnal route. The action is described in texts accompanying the individual hours of the night, but it is basically complete in the sequences of pictures. In some cases, such as in the tomb of Thutmose III, we find stick figures and cursive hieroglyphs, indicating that the pictures and words were copied onto the wall from a papyrus original and giving the impression of an unrolled papyrus scroll. The Opening of the Mouth ritual, which served to give life to a statue or the body of a deceased person, comprises as many as seventy-five scenes whose depictions of ritual actions and their accompanying texts can be understood as a sort of pictorial "broadsheet."

78.

Were there Egyptian universities?

Education in ancient Egypt was basically a privilege of elite males, who were taught Egyptian cultural knowledge and the writing system. We do not know what education was received by the few attested women who were literate, or by women who rose to the few higher positions that were available to them, such as priestess of Hathor or God's Wife of Amun (see also **Question 92**). In the Old Kingdom, the state administration remained in the hands of the royal family until Dynasty 4, when it was expanded, professionalized, and supplemented by a provincial administration in areas distant from the residence. During this time education must have taken place primarily at the royal Residence. The circle of architects, master builders, and artists who were responsible for the major royal building projects, especially the pyramid complexes and the private cemeteries, would have been trained in the theory and practice of their professions. As in later times, this training probably occurred in workshops, but since the Middle Kingdom it also took place in families, where professional knowledge was passed on from father to son (see also **Question 62**).

The classic bureaucratic state of the Middle Kingdom developed a system of education in which prospective "scribes"—civil servants with a basic knowledge of reading and writing—were trained through the use of special school texts. These spanned a variety of genres, including "instructional" texts, which were devoted especially to correct ethical behavior, literary and religious texts, model letters, and administrative and legal documents. Scribal education focused on the cursive scripts as opposed to the hieroglyphs used on monuments, and it made particular use of writing from dictation and learning important texts by heart. School exercises and schoolboy manuscripts, often replete with spelling errors, are attested in large numbers from the New Kingdom, a period for which actual schools are archaeologically attested. Called "houses of instruction" by the ancient Egyptians, they have been found in the workmen's settlement of Deir el-Medina, and in the temple complexes of the Ramesseum, Deir el-Bahari, and the Mut temple. The teaching of language (grammatical exercises are attested in Demotic school texts), rhetoric, and ethics was complemented by basic training in mathematics and book-keeping, as well as geographical and cultural knowledge about Egypt. At least from the New Kingdom onwards, this basic schooling was followed by specialized training, once the student chose one of the three careers that were open to him: state administration, the priesthood, or the military. Preparation for the military began with physical training (a stela of King Taharqa mentions a long-distance run of soldiers jogging from Memphis to the Faiyum), and went on to include familiarity with types of weaponry and knowledge of tactics and strategy. In the New Kingdom a center for military training, attended also by royal princes, was located at the naval port of Memphis called Perunefer ("Beautiful Departure"), and the recent excavations at the Ramesside capital of Pi-Ramesses in the eastern Delta have brought to light a sort of military academy with stables, workshops, and training facilities for chariot drivers (see **Questions 56** and **58**).

Some people have applied the term "university" to a special institution of Egyptian temples, the so-called "house of life" (*per-ankh*). This was the place where academic and literary texts were written and copied: theological texts, ritual books, funerary texts, medico-magical handbooks, and works of literature, as well as astronomical, geographical, and mathematical treatises. It was also the place where persons were trained for the priestly profession. In the temples of Egypt's later periods, texts constituting the cultural repertoire of Egypt were recorded on the walls on a large scale, thus establishing a canon of Egyptian civilization. A "house of life" was thus indeed a sort of academy worthy of being called a "university," as here an attempt was made to bring together a "totality" of knowledge (*universitas litterarum*).

 **79.**

Did the Egyptians solve crossword puzzles?

From the period of Dynasties 18 to 20, we have some extraordinary inscriptions that Egyptologists have come to call "Egyptian crossword puzzles." They consist of horizontal and vertical lines of texts divided into equal squares that can be read both across the rows and down the columns. The top line of a stela now in the British Museum with hymns to the goddess Mut advises the reader to even read the stela as many as "three times," with the third direction probably being an angular "spiral" from the outside inwards. In this manner, increasingly briefer horizontal and vertical portions of the two original hymns combined to form a third hymn. This crossword puzzle exploits the fact that many hieroglyphs can be read not only as phonetic signs, but also as ideograms or as (unpronounced) determinatives—that is, signs that indicate a word's category of meaning (see also **Question 72**). By way of example: the hieroglyph depicting the "floor plan" of a one-room house can be read, or understood, as the ideogram for *pr* "house," a phonetic sign for the consonant sequence *p* + *r* (as in the verb *pri* "to go out"), or an indication of the category of meaning following a word such as "tomb", which was seen as a house for the dead. Thus, depending on the direction of reading, signs or groups of signs allowed for different ways of how they could—and should—be read. The challenge of making it possible to read each text square correctly in two different ways forced the text's author to use sequences of relatively brief divine epithets that sometimes seem artificial compared to normal hymns.

Different languages or scripts could also be employed. From the late Ptolemaic era, for example, we have the stela of a man named Moschion, created for the purpose of thanking Osiris for curing a foot condition; it takes the form of a crossword puzzle in which the cure is described in both Greek and Demotic. However, crossword hymns are not just to be taken as games, but rather as theological attempts to illustrate the manifold divine nature of the deities worshipped through the inscriptions, while at the same time concealing insight into a specific deity's theology from the uninitiated (see **Question 52**).

 **80.**

What do we know about
ancient Egyptian music?

Many musical instruments known from the ancient Near East have been recreated and the replicas played. But in 1939, the two original trumpets found in the intact tomb of Tutankhamun, which are made from silver and copper, were played again for the first time after more than 3,000 years. In a BBC broadcast from the Egyptian museum at Cairo (the recording of which can be found at the BBC website), trumpeter James Tappern played them, and their sound had an astonishing quality. However, he had to play modern tunes because in ancient Egypt there was no system of musical notation and thus genuinely ancient Egyptian melodies are unknown.

While trumpets were mainly used in the Egyptian army, other musical instruments were used more widely. Among the more simple Egyptian instruments were those of the percussion family—clappers, castagnets, sistrums (Figure 14), and different varieties of drums. Wind instruments such as flutes, double-clarinets, and double-oboi were also common, as were string instruments like lyres, lutes, and different varieties of the harp. Representations of musicians and singers performing their craft are not uncommon, especially in tomb scenes, though these depictions are always selective and subject to artistic convention and decorum. Nonetheless, from tomb depictions we can infer that instruments were often played in ensembles of several musicians, accompanied by singers. Musicians were employed in the temple cult and in rituals, but also performed in the secular sphere, at banquets and likely in funerary processions. Texts and depictions also attest to a wide variety of songs (some of them sung alternatingly by two groups of singers), as well as different dances. Music was also a means to pacify ferocious deities, and to ward off demons. This importance of music is well expressed in a hymn for Hathor, the goddess of the sky and of love, and a patroness of music, that King Antef II in the First Intermediate Period had inscribed on a stele:

> O you gods of the Western sky, O you who rule the shore of the Western sky, who rejoice at Hathor's coming, who love to see her beauty rise: I let her know, I say at her side that I rejoice in seeing her. My hands do [the gesture] 'come to me, come to me!', my body says, my lips repeat: Holy music for Hathor, music a million times, because you love music, million times music to your *ka* [the living forces] wherever you are. I am he who makes the singer waken music for Hathor, every day at any hour she wishes. May your heart be at peace with music, may you proceed in goodly peace, may you rejoice in life and gladness with the Horus who loves you [the king].

Figure 14: Two royal women of the time of
King Amenophis III (*c.*1370 BCE) each wearing a
sistrum. Limestone relief from Western Thebes

 **81.**

Did the Egyptians read Homer?

To date, we have more than 2,000 ancient manuscripts of the Homeric epics, the *Iliad* and the *Odyssey*, ranging in date from the third century BCE to the seventh century BCE, including many hundreds of manuscript fragments from Egypt. Among the latter, the *Iliad* is by far more often attested than the *Odyssey*. Knowledge of Homer was thus widespread in Graeco-Roman Egypt. But the real question is whether the Homeric epics had any real influence on Egyptian literature (see also **Question 74**), and whether we can see any indication of a reciprocal influence on Greek literary genres, such as the novel.

At the center of this debate is a special group of Demotic texts, the "epics" of the Petubastis cycle (so-called after a figure who appears in the texts). These texts idealize the Libyan Period (945–742 BCE) as a time of military prowess. The texts are evidently derived from written and oral tales that grew up around important figures of the Libyan Period, transmitting historically correct information about the seventh century BCE down into the Graeco-Roman era. The most important epics are the *Contest for the Benefice of Amun*, in which a priest of Horus from Buto struggles to obtain his rightful office and income of high priest of Amun of Karnak, and the *Contest for the Breastplate of Inaros*, in which several heroes and their armies battle for possession of the breastplate of Inaros, the (Libyan) prince of Heliopolis. Like Homer's *Iliad*, these two texts belong to the genre of aristocratic heroic poetry. With the *Iliad*, they share the central theme of testing men through battle, which ends either in triumph or doom. All three texts also stress courage, self-confidence, and physical strength as the important qualities of heroes, and emphasize their weapons and armor as indispensable status symbols of a hero-warrior. The target audience for the Egyptian epics may have been the professional soldiers in the Egyptian army, who would have been keenly interested in chivalry, honor and loyalty, prestige objects, and tournament-like, regulated combat. For soldiers, this type of heroic poetry could have served as literature that at the same time provided them with identity and entertainment (see also **Question 75**). Since we thus far lack Egyptian precursors for this sort of heroic poetry, knowledge of the *Iliad* could have prompted the written elaboration of oral tales. In a third text, however, the Struggle of Petekhons against Sarpot, Queen of the land of women, the two protagonists fall in love and join in combat against the prince of India. By focusing on love and adventure (apart from deeds of war), this story represents a transition to the genre of the novel, and, along with a number of other Egyptian texts, gives rise to the suspicion that the Greek novel might have been originally stimulated by Egyptian texts.

82.

What literary influence did ancient Egypt have on the Old Testament?

Ever since Egyptian texts became widely known in the second half of the nineteenth century, scholars began searching for ancient Egyptian parallels to biblical texts. At first, their goal was to confirm the scripture, while later it was to situate the Bible in the wider cultural context of the Near East. A significant Egyptian influence can be detected in genres and literary motifs of the Old Testament. Scholars also assume Egyptian influences on the Psalms, Ecclesiastes (Koheleth), the priestly creation story, and other texts. Often, however, these texts and motifs have been compared with the easily accessible (for modern readers) texts from the Egyptian New Kingdom, when what should actually be consulted is the literature of ancient Egypt's later periods.

In the literature of Egypt's Late Period (664–332 BCE) we find clear parallels to motifs in the oft-cited Psalm 104, the Song of Songs, and the book of Job. Perhaps the best-known example can be seen in Proverbs 22.17–23.14, which borrows from the Instruction of Amenemope, a wisdom text in circulation at least as late as Dynasty 26—that is, the sixth century BCE. The atmosphere and character of the Egyptian Late Period is clearly visible in the descriptions of the story of Joseph and Israel's stay in Egypt, where there are also similar literary motifs, as, for example, the contest between Moses and Pharaoh's magicians (Exodus 7) and the similar contest between Siosire and the Ethiopian magicians in the Demotic cycle of Setne-Khaemwese. In addition, the criticisms directed at kings in the books of Chronicles find parallels in Egyptian "apocalyptic" works (see **Question 37**).

Numerous religious concepts also have Egyptian parallels: man as God's image, the concept of God as shepherd, the weighing of the heart (see **Question 39**), the forming of men on a potter's wheel, the discovery of sacred books in order to legitimize religious reform (see **Question 6**), and so forth. The Hebrew of the Old Testament also displays a certain Egyptian influence in the area of vocabulary and idioms: for instance, "face between his knees" in the story of Elijah; the expression "standing and sitting" in the sense of "comport oneself"; the term "way of life"; the comparison of the prophet Jeremiah with a "bronze wall'; "burning coals on the head" as a metaphor for penitence; and the designation of God as "sun of righteousness." These literary and linguistic borrowings are part of a much wider cultural influence that Egypt had on Israel, as has been pointed out in recent decades by Othmar Keel and his students. In addition to textual borrowings, this influence is found in imagery as well, and is especially clear in the iconographic material from Palestine, in particular, representations on seals. One example of Egyptian influence is apparent in the solar symbolism of Yahweh belief in Israel and Judah during the eighth century BCE, which incorporated the Egyptian sundisk and Uraeus serpents.

7

Egyptian Society

83.

Who was an ancient Egyptian?

According to the Greek historian Herodotus (*c.*450 BCE), an oracle of the god Amun once responded to a question by saying: "Egypt was all the land that the Nile watered in its course," and that "those were Egyptians who, dwelling below the city of Elephantine, drank from the water of the Nile" (*Histories*, book 2, chap. 18). Egyptian ideology contrasted Egypt, the land of culture and order (*Maat*; see **Question 39**), to foreign lands—that is, to the world of disorder and chaos (*isfet*). The Egyptian word for "human" also meant "Egyptian," as in the representation of the four human races (Egyptians, Asiatics, Libyans, and Nubians) in the Book of Gates, which dates to the New Kingdom. But whoever lived on Egyptian territory and spoke Egyptian was ideologically (if not necessarily sociologically) viewed as part of Egyptian culture. In fact, we can seldom recognize foreign persons and groups in the ancient sources, for as a rule, they quickly acculturated. It is only from the New Kingdom on that persons more frequently displayed their foreign background, as in the case of Maiherpri, a Nubian courtier who even received the privilege of a tomb in the Valley of the Kings, or as in the case of the Phoenician-Egyptian priest Khahap in the third century BCE. Such persons were socially and professionally integrated and doubtless viewed as assimilated Egyptians, though they also chose to retain elements of their culture of origin.

Interestingly, the Egyptian term "foreigner" was never applied to persons living in Egypt, but only to foreigners beyond the borders—that is, to those who were entirely alien, and beyond any possibility of adopting the Egyptian way of life. Acculturation usually occurred within the frameworks of the family, the workplace, and the locale where people resided, though there is also some evidence of state encouragement of acculturation. On the other hand, the notion of "foreignness" could begin just beyond one's own home town—"strangers" from a different settlement could be identified as foreign in the texts. This is likely due to the cultural and linguistic differences that existed between the different parts of Egypt. For example, in the Story of Sinuhe, which dates to Dynasty 12, the protagonist feels himself in Palestine "as if a Delta-man saw himself in Elephantine [Egypt's southern border]." Similarly, in a satirical text from the New Kingdom, a scribe's allegedly disastrous writing is said to be "like the talk of a man of the Delta with a man of Elephantine."

 **84.**

Was there racism in ancient Egypt?

According to widespread opinion, in ancient Egypt there is no evidence of explicit discrimination or persecution of persons of non-Egyptian ethnic or religious affiliations. Immanuel Geiss, an expert in the history of racism, has gone so far as to call pharaonic Egypt the "most ancient and impressive example for refuting racist theories." When Egyptian sources depict foreigners as representatives of barbarism and chaos, these are always persons outside Egypt, not immigrants into Egypt, who quickly became acculturated (see **Question 83**). In the New Kingdom, if not earlier, ethnicity was even a positive trait that a person could vaunt, and which did not entail professional or social disadvantage. Such generalizations do not mean that there were never tensions between established residents and immigrants, but we have so far no evidence of discrimination or persecution by the state, the priesthood, or ordinary people prior to the first millennium BCE. It is difficult to find examples of pejorative remarks in ancient Egyptian texts, and when we do, there may well be non-racist explanations. For example, in a letter from the Middle Kingdom workmen's village of Illahun, we find the isolated remark, "Send 30 workmen to accompany the [...]. Do not send me these Asiatics!" While the reason for this statement escapes us, it can be observed that during the Middle Kingdom, Asiatics were a growing part of the cultural fabric, and were often valued for their particular expertise in, for example, viticulture and the textile industry. And in the New Kingdom, King Amenhotep II advised his friend, the viceroy of Nubia, "Beware of its [*i.e.*, Nubia's] people and their sorcerors"—Nubian magic was feared, but not Nubians as such, who were an important part of the Egyptian military system. Egypt was presumably a more open society than has often been stated, though today, we can barely catch a glimpse of the multicultural spectacle that must have existed in the large cities at the very least of the second and first millennia BCE, though even elsewhere in Egypt there were individuals and groups of non-Egyptian origin in every period (see **Question 70**).

 **85.**

Why did the ancient Egyptians not have words meaning "uncle" and "aunt"?

Systems of kinship terms are culture-specific and vary considerably. Compared to modern western languages (even English, which has fewer terms than what was used in the Old English period), the ancient Egyptian language had an extremely restricted number of kinship terms. There were basically only six words—father, mother, son, daughter, brother, sister—that is, the terms appropriate to the framework of a nuclear family (as well as "husband" and "wife"). Also attested, though infrequently, are "father-in-law" and "mother-in-law." This core group of terms was used with broader meanings in daily communication. Thus the words for "brother" and "sister" often designated all collateral relatives, including uncle, nephew, cousin, and brother-in-law, and aunt, niece, (female) cousin, and sister-in-law, respectively. The terms for "father" and "mother" occasionally occur for earlier generations of a lineage (grandfather/grandmother), and they were also used for "stepfather/stepmother," while those for "son" and "daughter" sometimes designate linear descendants of later generations (grandson/granddaughter), as well as stepson/stepdaughter. In addition to these extended usages, texts (but not salutations!) could express exact relationships by a combination of basic terms, such as "the mother of the mother of his mother" = "his great-grandmother" and "the son of the sister of the mother of his mother" = "his first cousin once removed." Finally, there was no terminological distinction between patrilineage and matrilineage in ancient Egypt, and kinship was almost always expressed in relation to the central figure of a text or depiction.

![ibis] 86.

Why did elite Egyptians not wear beards?

Whether or not men wear beards is determined by cultural traditions, religious requirements, changes in style, or professional regulations. Statuettes from the Predynastic art of the Upper Egyptian Naqada I–II culture (3500–3300 BCE)— for example, the so-called MacGregor Man in the Ashmolean Museum, Oxford, and a figure now in Brussels—wear a long, full beard that reaches the chest; and other representations from that period also show men with beards (Figure 15). In the classical Merimda culture of Lower Egypt, men are depicted with beards as early as 4500 BCE. We have from this period a clay head meant to be fastened to the top of a staff, where holes in the chin indicate that beard hairs were once attached to it. This Predynastic predilection for beards came to an end after 3000 BCE, and was replaced by the shaved chin that was now a cultural and status convention for male elite, while wearing wigs (on intentionally shaved heads) became the norm for elite men and women. At this time, an artificially stylized and idealized appearance was imposed on the natural human form (see also **Questions 53** and **54**). The only thing still allowed was the mustache. From this time on, full beards were seen as a mark of uncivilized behavior or lower social rank, confined in use to ordinary people and foreigners (including genuinely foreign gods, such as Sopdu). Among the often unconventional and humorous figurative ostraca (painted limestone chips; see also **Question 91**) created by the men who worked on the tombs in the Valley of the Kings, we even have a depiction of a king with a stubble, and in the Theban tomb of a man named

Intef there is once the depiction of the tomb owner, fat and unshaven. The beards of the Predynastic Period seem to have had a continuation in stylized form in the ceremonial beards worn by Egyptian kings and gods—the royal straight beard that broadened from top to bottom and the braided divine beard that curved outwards at the lower end. Like his clothing and his insignia of office, the king's beard was a status symbol, attached to his head with straps. Even the great Sphinx of Giza, a representation of the king with a human face and lion body, originally sported a beard!

Figure 15: Bearded figure from Gebelein,
*c.*3500 BCE

 **87.**

Are Niankhkhnum and Khnumhotep the first attested gay couple?

When the mastaba of Niankhkhnum and Khnumhotep was discovered under the causeway leading to the pyramid of Unas in 1964, Egyptologists were faced not only with its unusually careful depiction of flora and fauna, but also with its unprecedented flaunting of the affection of two men for one another. Although the decoration of the tomb also includes the families (wives and children) of both persons, the men are depicted embracing not their wives, but one another. Both men were priests in the funerary cult of the deceased King Niuserre and "chief manicurists" of the ruling king, thus explaining their high status; they had the privilege of touching the power-laden, divine body of their monarch. Many scenes in this double tomb depict the brothers together or have parallels to one another on the opposite walls. The images include the transport of their statues, the deceased in front of an offering table, fishing and fowling, shipbuilding, professional scenes with manicurists, pedicurists and barbers, market scenes with a "police monkey," inspections of the harvest, artisans at work, the butchery of animals, and the life of shepherds. In the antechamber and in two places in the offering chamber, Niankhkhnum and Khnumhotep are depicted embracing one another in the presence of all their children. Their noses are touching one another, which in Egypt was tantamount to kissing. We have no other scene demonstrating this sort of intimacy between men, and seldom do we see such scenes even in connection with married men and women, or mother and child—even in the art of the Amarna Period (see **Question 64**). There are other unusual scenes as well. In the passageway to the open court, Niankhkhnum and Khnumhotep each sit in a tub-shaped chair harnessed to two donkeys. The antechamber contains two scenes in which the conductor of a small orchestra announces the "Song of the Two Divine Brothers"—the two men are evidently being compared to Horus and Seth, and a festival is being staged for them. Niankhkhnum and Khnumhotep are also depicted jointly above the text of their contract with the priests who will handle their funerary cult.

Scholars were at first of the opinion that these were twins, with the slight preference accorded to Niankhkhnum in the tomb possibly indicating that he was the first-born of the two. An alternative hypothesis proposed to identify these representations as the world's earliest depiction of a gay couple. This is not likely to be the case. While homosexuality is attested in ancient Egypt (from depictions on ostraca to literary texts), it was not a socially accepted form of sexuality, and its prominent and eternal display in the Old Kingdom does not seem feasible. The most recent explanation, set forth by David O'Connor, is that Niankhkhnum and Khnumhotep were conjoined (Siamese) twins. This would explain why they had the same profession, their shared ownership of the tomb, and the way in which they are depicted together in the tomb, with Niankhkhnum always to the right of Khnumhotep or on the west/south wall. Even their names may be a reflection of their conjoined existence: the name of the creator god Khnum has the same sequence of consonants as the verb "to join," and in the tomb, the two names follow one another in such a way that the two elements "Khnum" are juxtaposed, as though the two men were in fact joined to one another. Their joint offering foundation and the single burial festival could also indicate that the two died at the same time, as is in fact inevitable with Siamese twins. Only in the rock-cut chamber, evidently in exact agreement with the position of the sarcophagi lying in the burial chamber just below, is their depiction switched, with Niankhkhnum shown on the left and Khnumhotep on the right wall. Was this done deliberately, so as to reverse the positions they had occupied throughout their lives and thus allow the two brothers freedom of movement in the afterlife?

 **88.**

How rich was Tutankhamun?

Nowadays the most famous of all Egyptian Kings, Tutankhamun was of little historical importance, and after his untimely death he received nothing more than a relatively modest emergency burial in the Valley of the Kings. But today, thanks to the fact that the entrance to his tomb was covered over before it could be plundered, he is the epitome of Egyptian splendor and riches. As pharaoh, Tutankhamun was lord of the land and thus, at least ideologically, the sole owner of Egypt and its resources. In reality, by his reign in late Dynasty 18, the temples had established themselves as practically independent economic entities within the state, and even members of the elite had considerable private property and privileges (see also **Question 29**). Nevertheless, we can say that until the end of the New Kingdom the king had almost unlimited riches; it was after this, at the turn of the first millennium, that he experienced a precipitous loss of status.

A simple calculation based on administrative documents and accounts reveals in a striking way the gigantic difference between the king and ordinary Egyptians at the end of the New Kingdom. At that time, a simple workman or artisan received a monthly wage amounting to the value of 7 units of copper (see **Question 29**)—that is, 1.5 sacks of barley and 4 sacks of emmer (wheat). A foreman or a simple scribe received only a little more, 9.5 units of copper, while a servant-girl received considerably less, only 4.5 units. How small such an income was is shown by its buying power: for 10 units of copper, one could purchase 5 sacks of barley or 2 pairs of leather sandals or 1 bedsheet or 1 simple wooden box. We are thus at the very bottom of society. In contrast, the income of a seal-bearer—that is, a middle-level state bureaucrat—amounted to up to 190 copper units monthly (equaling between 77 and 95 sacks of barley)—about 20 times more! For simple people, the wish for a burial in a coffin or even a private tomb was hopeless from the start: the wood for a coffin cost about 100 units of copper, its manufacture up to 20 units, and if it was to be painted and inscribed the cost was another 20 units. For a simple workman, artisan, or ordinary scribe, a painted coffin amounted to about 20 months' income and thus basically could not be afforded. The cost of a simple tomb would have far exceeded the entire amount he would have earned in a lifetime (which was usually brief, see **Question 89**). What a contrast to the buying power of a middle-level bureaucrat, for whom a coffin cost less than a month's income, to say nothing about the income of a high-ranking official! In this comparison, where did Tutankhamun stand? The most costly of the nearly 6,000 objects in his tomb treasure (which was doubtless one of the most modest) was his inner coffin of solid gold, which weighed 110 kilograms. In the New Kingdom, gold was worth 200 times more than copper. The worth of the coffin thus corresponded to 22,000 kilograms of copper, or 242,000 units of copper—that is, an ordinary artisan's wages for 35,000 months or about 3,000 years. And this is only the value of the metal—it does not include the manufacturing of the coffin and its decoration!

89.

How long did one live in ancient Egypt?

The average life expectancy at birth was about 30–35 years in ancient Egypt, though it could vary considerably according to regional or social conditions. For example, in the east Delta city of Avaris, the Hyksos capital (see **Questions 32 and 56**), skeletons from around 1550 BCE indicate an average lifespan of just over 18.5 years. An extremely high child mortality rate contributed to the statistically low life expectancy. But those who reached adulthood had a good chance of attaining even a high old age, and the chances were far greater for the upper strata of society, who had a more balanced diet, better medical care and hygiene, and did less physical labor. A king like Ramesses II lived to about 90, and Pepy II might even have lived past the age of 100, close to the (probably almost never attained) Egyptian ideal lifetime of 110 years: 10 years of childhood and 100 years as a youth and an adult.

A drastic but probably quite realistic depiction of a peasant's life is given in a text called the "Satire of the Trades" (see **Question 96** for the text). Until the 1940s, living conditions for most people in Egypt remained what they were in antiquity, and even today, they are often not dissimilar: housing consisted of simple huts of mud or mud brick, with only one windowless room and a floor of trodden dirt. Animals lived nearly side-by-side with people, whose immediate environment was thus fouled by garbage, dung (which was gathered by the children and used as fuel), and human feces; and everywhere, there were vermin, parasites, rats, and mice. By contrast, elite Egyptians lived in veritable villas, some of them with sanitary facilities. For example, upper-class houses at Tell el-Amarna had a bathroom with a stone tub and a separate toilet with a toilet seat.

There was typically a high seasonal mortality rate, especially during the annual "plague of the year" that followed the Nile inundation (see **Question 91**). Some of the known illnesses in ancient Egypt were diarrhea (including amoebic dysentery), typhus, malaria, tuberculosis, smallpox (known from the mummy of Ramesses V), pneumonic plague, polio (known from a stela depicting a priest named Rama with a crippled foot and from the mummy of King Siptah), schistosomiasis (in the 1950s, 95 percent of the peasants in Egypt still contracted this disease), hepatitis, guinea worm disease and other illnesses caused by worms, conjunctivitis, malnutrition, diphtheria, dermatological conditions, and tumors. Also well-attested are fractures of all sorts, and injuries to the skull and the spinal column. Since the flour used in baking bread was ground coarsely and mixed with sand, teeth were often worn down to the nerve, which could lead to painful abscesses, but there is hardly any attestation of cavities!

90.

Did ancient Egyptians get married?

Quite unlike today, ancient Egypt had no formalized marriage authenticated by a legal document, nor did it have any civil or religious ceremony. Instead, marriage seems to have been established simply by cohabitating and starting a family. There is thus no special term for marriage; the texts mostly talk of the founding of a household, or they state that a man took a wife for himself. An equally private matter was divorce (for which there is also no term), which meant the departure of one of the spouses from their dwelling and the division of their common property. Divorce was not burdened by social stigma, and not only was remarriage common, it was in most cases necessary to assure existence. While the couple could dispose freely of the goods brought into the marriage so long as they remained together, when divorce occurred, the goods acquired jointly during the marriage were divided up, with the husband receiving two-thirds and the wife one-third. Beginning in the Third Intermediate Period, there were various types of marriage documents that did not authenticate the marriage itself, but rather dealt with financial arrangements and support obligations. Adultery was viewed as a threat to the marriage, in all likelihood not because of the unfaithfulness, but because further progeny jeopardized the family property—illegitimate children counted as children of the couple every bit as much as legitimate children, and they had inheritance rights. If there were no children, adoption was a possibility, and one that was often taken to ensure that after death funerary rituals were carried out properly and the funerary cult maintained—two duties marking one as a rightful heir (see **Question 76**).

Brother-sister marriages are only seldom attested among private people, and while they were somewhat common in the case of kings, they were not necessarily consummated and heirs were most often produced out of unions between kings and women of their harem. Among non-royals, there are also no certain cases of polygamy; all suspected examples—such as the mention of several wives on funerary stelae—could also be explained through successive marriages. But kings often had several wives, including the "great king's wife" (*i.e.*, chief wife), who was herself usually of royal descent, but could also come from a "bourgeois" family (as in the case of Teye, the mother of Akhenaten), or from a foreign royal court (as with Mentuhotep II's Nubian wives or Thutmose III's Asiatic ones).

 **91.**

Did the Egyptians celebrate Carnival?

In western tradition—from the Roman Saturnalia to the Carnival customs of the European Middle Ages and the modern period—Carnival has been a festival in which, for one day, distinctions of rank are abolished and the world is topsy-turvy. But Carnivalesque customs exist throughout the world. From ancient Egypt, illustrated papyri and ostraca depict the world turned upside down: the "pharaoh" of the mice and his army attack the fortress of the cats; mice have cats for servants; a lion and an ibex play a board game with one another; a traveling animal orchestra of predatory animals and their prey (donkey, lion, crocodile, monkey) strike up a tune, a rhinoceros sits on a treetop instead of a swallow. On a papyrus in Turin, the verso is comprised of such animal scenes, while the recto contains scenes of sexual acts performed by an old bald man and a lady of high society. These might also be illustrations of the abolishment of the normal order of things.

These types of scenes might be tied to the Egyptian New Year festival, which marked a dangerous calendrical transition that has been feared in many cultures. Even today, German-speaking people speak of the period between Christmas and the New Year as the time "between the years," which folk belief viewed as a threatening time. In Egypt, the beginning of the year was originally correlated with the annual Nile inundation (see **Question 1**). This was followed by the "plague of the year," for which Sakhmet, goddess of war and plague, was responsible. The Greek historian Herodotus and a Demotic poem describe music and dance, sexual excesses, and alcoholic

binges during the festival in honor of the goddess Bastet in
Bubastis. This goddess, who could manifest herself as a cat,
was the peaceful aspect of the wild lion goddess Sakhmet
(and was also identified with Mut, the consort of Amun), who
constantly had to be pacified. In the Book of the Heavenly
Cow, humankind, who had revolted against the sun god, was
supposed to be annihilated by Sakhmet, until Re decided to
have mercy on them. To prevent the annihilation, the fields
were flooded with red-colored beer that looked like blood—
Sakhmet drank it, became intoxicated, and calmed down. In the
temple of Mut at Luxor, archaeologists have recently identified
a "porch of drunkenness," and a festival of drunkenness that
took place there. The concept of pacifying divine beings with
alcohol is older than this, however. During the Old Kingdom
work gangs were labeled "How drunk is Khufu" (Mycerinus,
Sahure, *etc.*), probably intended to pacify the raging and godlike
king of that name. It is thus conceivable that on New Year's
day (the first month of the Egyptian calendar was originally
called "drunkenness") there might have been a festival with
Carnivalesque traits whose aim was to pacify the dangerous
goddess Sakhmet.

92.

Did ancient Egyptian women have equal rights?

"You have given women the same power as men!" Using this statement from a well-known invocation of the goddess Isis from the second century CE, an Egyptologist in 1950 characterized the status of women in ancient Egypt as exceptionally privileged and possessing equal rights with men. Now that gender history has reached Egyptology and some female scholars have devoted themselves to this theme from a female perspective, a more nuanced assessment has emerged, one that takes into account the specifics of the texts that have survived to us, changes over time, and different social milieus (Figure 16). It also accounts for archaeological evidence. For instance, investigation of burials at Old Kingdom Elephantine has revealed that many women suffered fractures of the lower arm, an indication of domestic violence: they had evidently raised an arm in front of their face to protect themselves from physical abuse by their husbands. In all periods of ancient Egyptian history, women were legally and financially independent: they owned property, could make legal complaints, buy and sell, inherit and bequeath, make wills, and testify as witnesses in legal proceedings. Education (see **Question 78**), however, was something they could at best obtain privately and unofficially. Their low literacy rate might be one of the reasons why women often asked male relatives to represent them in legal and financial matters. With few exceptions, positions in state administration and the priesthoods were barred to women; their firmly established roles were caring for the family and managing the household, though they were also common in certain branches of skilled labor, such as textile and food production. Priestly offices were largely reserved for men. Prior to the New Kingdom, women played a part in the cult of the goddess Hathor, and in practically no other, while from the New Kingdom onward, they could never be priestesses and were at best singers in the temples. We do, however, see upper-class women occupying themselves with the management of estates.

Women belonging to the royal family had much more latitude in their activities. The position of royal mother was an important one; they and the king's wives could even act as regents and were doubtless informally involved in political decisions. Recent finds from the Old Kingdom indicate that in that period women could hold the highest state office, that of vizier. We also know of three queens who assumed kingship: Sobeknofru, Hatshepsut, and Twosre. It is especially interesting to see how the tension between the male role of the kingly office and the female identity of Hatshepsut influenced her depiction in sculpture. While at first her images portray an extremely feminine rendering with attributes of royalty added on, her depiction became increasingly masculine, until finally she was shown as a traditional male king, though the texts leave no doubt whatsoever as to her feminine identity. In the New Kingdom and later, another important political and religious office assumed by women of the royal family was that of "God's Wife of Amun" at Thebes, the holder of which also had access to a great deal of wealth. The principally unequal status of women, however, is confirmed by the archaeological evidence, which reveals that burials of men were usually richer than those of women.

Figure 16: Wooden figure of a woman carrying offerings, from a Theban tomb of the early Middle Kingdom, around 1950 BCE

93.

How many people lived in ancient Egypt?

Insight into settlement and population geography is essential to our understanding of Egyptian history. Political power is based on control over people and economic resources. It is extremely difficult, however, to supply reliable information regarding the population of Egypt prior to the Graeco-Roman Period, for we have no true census data. Our earliest precise figures are from the Greek historian Diodorus Siculus, *c.*60 BCE (and, later, Flavius Josephus), who speaks of 3 million in his own time and 7 million "in earlier times," and of 300,000 "free inhabitants" of Alexandria, though the total must have been at least 500,000. He estimates the number of "villages and towns" as 18,000 "in former times," which resembles Herodotus' figure of 20,000 "densely populated towns." Modern demographic research on ancient Egypt has employed a whole range of methods to arrive at a population figure: considerations regarding the yield of the cultivable land, statistics derived from cemeteries, extrapolation of population figures from the number of known settlements, and assumptions regarding age and fertility, as well as regarding birth, death, and growth rates (see also **Question 89**). Even so, only very rough estimates are possible, and yield a population of about 4 million for the New Kingdom. In the Old Kingdom, when cities were small, the provincial capitals must have had only 500–2,000 inhabitants, and Memphis as the capital, some 15,000. The gradual growth of cities can be estimated based on the situation in the New Kingdom. A metropolis like Memphis must have had at its peak about 150,000 inhabitants, while large cities such as Thebes, Amarna, and Heliopolis had perhaps 50,000, and provincial centers about 5,000 (see also **Question 58**). Most of the population, however, lived in the countryside in hundreds of little villages that were likely each home to only a handful of families.

 **94.**

Did ancient Egypt have
a legal system?

Diodorus Siculus listed the Persian King Darius I as the sixth and last of Egypt's lawgivers. Although the first five lawgivers of Egypt preceding him in this list are probably for the most part legendary, according to a Demotic text, Darius, in the interest of administering the satrapy of Egypt according to native law, did indeed order a compilation of the laws of Egypt down through Dynasty 26 (which had immediately preceded the Persian conquest of the land). These were to be written down in both Demotic and in Aramaic translation so that the literate native inhabitants and their conquerors could read them (see also **Question 71**). Portions of law collections, perhaps copies of the Persian compilation or maybe also its successors, are attested from the Ptolemaic Period. Although we do not have direct evidence of the existence of earlier collections of laws, from the Middle Kingdom on, we do have mention of the names of laws. New Kingdom textual references to the doing of something "according to the law" lead us to suspect that prior to the Persian Period there must already have been compilations of laws available for consultation. These could have been kept in the office of the vizier, the highest state official, who was the immediate subordinate of the king and responsible for legal matters. Actual laws are preserved in royal decrees of the New Kingdom. The Decree of Haremhab, for instance, mentions legal instructions regarding acts such as unlawful confiscation of boats and slaves, theft of leather hides, unlawful taxation of private fields, fraud in the calculation of lawful taxes, and the extortion of local mayors by officials who organized the annual participation of the king in the Opet festival at Thebes. Most of the ancient laws, however, must be inferred from the documentation of actual legal cases, which record not only the applicable ruling for the crime, but also sometimes cite precedents.

 # 95.

What do we know about prostitution in ancient Egypt?

In Book II of his *Histories*, Herodotus relates that King Khufu forced his own daughter into prostitution to get money to build his pyramid—clearly a late legend that tallies with this king's bad reputation in the Graeco-Roman Period. Yet, just a few years ago, a French Egyptologist actually went so far as to claim that Herodotus' account was not to be believed for the simple reason that there were no bordellos in Old Kingdom Egypt! But quite certainly there was prostitution in the pyramid age. Prior to the Ptolemaic Period, however, the sources contain only a small number of explicit references to it. These especially take the form of warnings in instructional texts, in which teachers warn their pupils—future administrative or military officials—not to frequent shady parts of the city and involve themselves with prostitutes. Along with "streetwalkers" and "women of pleasure," texts also use extremely vulgar and pejorative terms like "filthy cunt." For other phrases, such as "woman of the outside," it has been questioned whether the reference might be to prostitutes who would have plied their trade outside the town walls. In contrast to other ancient cultures, Egypt's official literature evidently displays a certain reluctance to address this theme.

 **96.**

Why was Egypt's "working class" never praised?

Though agriculture was the basis of ancient Egyptian civilization and thus the basis of the existence of the king and administrative elite (see **Question 29**), the enormous work effort invested in it by the majority of the population is scarcely ever mentioned in the texts, let alone treated with respect. Quite to the contrary, a Ramesside text called the "Satire of the Trades," which depicts the vocation of a scribe (the basic qualification for employment as a state official; see also **Question 78**) as the only one worth striving for, identifies the profession of the farmer as its outright antithesis:

> Let me expound to you the situation of the peasant, the other hard profession [*apart from that of the soldier*]. The water is high and he [*the peasant*] stands soaked on the bank. He must attend to his equipment. By day he cuts his farming tools; by night he twists rope. He equips himself to go to the field as if it were for a fight. The dried field lies before him; he goes out to get his team. Many days go by while he is after the herdsman, in order to get a team. He comes back with it and makes for it a track in the field. Comes dawn, he goes to make a start and does not find it in its place. He spends three days searching for it; he finds it in the bog. He finds no hides on them; the jackals have chewed them. He sets out, his garment in his hand, to beg for himself a team. When he finally reaches his field he finds (it) tramped down.

He spends time ploughing himself, and the caterpillar is after him. When he finishes the seed while sowing the soil, he thus will not see a green blade. He has to do three plowings with borrowed grain. His wife is forced to trade, but she does not find anything for barter. [...] Don't you remember the situation of the farmer during the registration of the crops? The caterpillar takes one half, the hippopotamus eats the rest. The mice are plenty in the field, the grasshoppers descend. The cattle eats away, and the sparrows steal: Woe to the farmer! As to the rest of it on the threshing floor, the thieves finish it off. The borrowed cattle is wrecked, the team is tired after all the threshing and ploughing. And then, the scribe lands on the shore in order to register the harvest. Attendants are behind him with batons, and policemen with clubs. One says: 'Give the grain!' He (says): 'There is none!' He is beaten savagely. He is bound, thrown in the well, submerged head down. His wife is bound in his presence. His children are in fetters. His laborers go away, they flee and abandon their grain.

We do, however, find idealized representations of the peasant's life in the tomb decoration of the elite, where socially elevated tomb owners, or even the king, are depicted performing agricultural work in the afterlife. These surely did not correspond to reality, but rather reflect the ease of living in the afterlife, when even hard manual labor could be performed effortlessly, or are vignettes meant to represent the deceased in the idyllic "Field of Rushes." The sole exception to the usual portrayal of farmers comes from a wisdom text of the sixth century BCE, now in the Brooklyn Museum, which states with deep respect: "The peasant is the highest of all callings; people serve him, his hands are their breath of life."

97.

Did the Egyptians live on nothing but bread and beer?

In the standardized offering prayers of the funerary monuments, bread and beer are always listed first: these were the two basic sources of nutrition for the Egyptian people. The two most common grains were emmer wheat and barley (see **Question 29**). In tomb decorations and on stelae we also see meats, vegetables, and fruits heaped up on the offering table in front of the deceased, and on the tables in the banquet scenes of the upper and middle classes. What we learn from texts and pictures can today be complemented by archaeobotanical and archaeozoological evidence: bones and plant remains from the refuse heaps of settlements, and also remains of food in the digestive tracts of mummies (see **Question 48**). The analysis of these remains provides not only a fuller picture of what the ancient Egyptians ate, but of who ate what. For example, wine, meat, honey, and spices, as well as exquisite cakes and sweets were expensive consumer items that were usually available only to the upper class. In the historical period, the meat animals were cattle, sheep, goats, and (especially in earlier times) deer, with beef and venison usually reserved for the elite. The importance of pigs, including as a convenient source of meat, has become clear in recent years (see **Question 47**). Apart from these meat animals, various kinds of birds, such as geese and ducks, chickens (which are mentioned for the first time in the reign of Thutmose III), partridges, quail, doves, and waterfowl were sources of protein, along with dozens of kinds of salt- and freshwater fish. Egyptians of all social strata, but especially those for whom meat was a rarity, ate vegetables, legumes, fruits, milk products, grains, eggs, and the pulp of various reed plants, and fruits—most often dates, but also sycamore figs, grapes, palm nuts, and carobs. Wine made from grapes was an elite beverage, though many probably drank other alcoholic beverages—for instance, date wine. Malnutrition was presumably most prevalent among the lower classes which have, as yet, been subject to little palaeopathological study. However, the recently excavated burials of workmen at Amarna demonstrate not only the effects of very hard physical labor, but also cases of malnutrition as the bodies displayed signs of iron deficiency.

 **98.**

Did the ancient Egyptians ever dress colorfully?

Reliefs and paintings in Egyptian tombs mostly depict people wearing white clothing; only seldom do we see colored or embroidered textiles. For this reason, scholars long held to the view that the Egyptians wore white most of the time. It has become clear, however, that these depictions were required by the tomb context which stressed the cleanliness and purity of the deceased and did not necessarily correspond to everyday textile reality (see also **Questions 53 and 54**). The tomb treasure of Tutankhamun included several dozen colorful garments, and remains of textiles from the plundered tomb of Thutmose IV show that Tutankhamun was no exception. In addition, a depiction of the "Window of Appearances" at Amarna shows the royal couple leaning on a lozenge-shaped cushion made of colored threads. This has compelled scholars to revise their opinion regarding, at the very least, the Dynasty 18 royal wardrobe and accoutrements, including not just garments and large cloths but also head coverings, belts and gloves, and even furniture. The designs include simple colored stripes, geometric shapes, and even complex ornamental patterns. Private tombs of Dynasty 18, and one horse burial that included a saddle cloth, also contained textiles with colored borders. Even the rubbish dump of the workmen's village at Amarna contained fragments of dyed linen—an indication that in Dynasty 18 the new fashions quickly penetrated all levels of society.

Linen was occasionally dyed red and yellow at the end of the Old Kingdom, but in the second millennium BCE Egyptian cloth manufacture was considerably influenced by the more advanced textile industry of the eastern Mediterranean (see **Question 16**). New methods of dyeing that appeared were making blue with indigo and red with madder, and violet or green double-dyeing. The Dynasty 20 "Satire of the Trades" (see also **Question 96**) describes the disadvantage of the profession of a tanner (who also used madder) and creator of shoe leather: "His hands are red with madder, like one who is smeared with his own blood."

Innovations in technology and new styles of fashion reached Egypt in various ways. In elite tombs, especially from the Middle and New Kingdoms, we see Levantines, Cretans, and Libyans depicted in their colorful native garb. There was always clothing among the gifts that rulers exchanged with one another. For example, the dowry sent by the Hurrian King Tushratta of Mitanni to Akhenaten included various garments and textiles—bringing Hurrian fashion to the Egyptian court. Textiles were often a part of the war booty brought back to Egypt, as in the case of Thutmose III's conquest of Megiddo, when Palestinian fashion was brought into Egypt. Large numbers of men and women specializing in textile manufacture were employed at the royal court, in the temples, and in private households. Immigration into Egypt and the exchange of goods and ideas furthered the introduction of new clothing styles and techniques of production. The new, colorful style included entire garments made of dyed yarns, or the clothing could have borders or wide bands sewn onto it. When first attested in Egypt, the new technique of weaving with colored yarn already had an astonishingly high level of quality, and it extended to a broad spectrum of applications: belts, head coverings, horse blankets, archery equipment from quivers to arm guards, gloves, curtains, pillowcases, banners, and so forth. Innovations in royal clothing also included new techniques of ornamentation: appliquéing with rosettes and sequins of gold and faïence, embroidery (on the tunic of Tutankhamun, with foreign motifs!), and appliquéd strips of cloth. A statuette of Amenhotep III depicts him in entirely Asiatic fashion: he stands clothed in a long Syrian robe with a fringed bottom, making a Mesopotamian gesture of prayer that is unparalleled in Egypt.

 **99.**

Did the ancient Egyptians practice sports and play games?

A ncient Egypt provides the richest evidence of any pre-Greek culture on sports, documented by texts and about 7,000 depictions (including dance, games, and hunting) mostly found in tomb reliefs and paintings. A royal stela of King Taharqa of the 25th Dynasty, dated to 685/684 BCE, is one of the most interesting documents in this respect. It speaks about the physical training of Egyptian soldiers, which culminated in a long-distance race over 100 kilometers: from Memphis to the Faiyum oasis and back to Memphis, with a break of two hours at the Faiyum. The entire distance took the runners about nine hours, and was rewarded by a common meal with the royal bodyguards and prizes. While the king accompanied the runners on his chariot for most of the distance, he also joined them in the race for a portion of the course. It is likely that since the Early Dynastic Period, if not before this, running was used to confirm the king's physical ability to rule. It became part of the royal jubilee festival (the so-called *Sed* festival) that reaffirmed the king's power after 30 years of reign (and then every third year), during which the king was expected to perform a race. In King Djoser's step pyramid precinct at Saqqara, built for the King's rule in the afterlife, distance markers of such a race are preserved in the South court (see also **Question 55**). Being an unrivaled sportsman with exceptional athletic abilities became a feature of royal display in the 18th Dynasty. Amenhotep II, whose archery practice with his tutor Min is depicted in Min's tomb, also boasts of his athletic prowess on his Great Sphinx Stele:

> There was not his like in this numerous army. Not one among them could draw his bow; he could not be approached in running. With strong arms, untiring when he took the oar, he rowed at the stern of his falcon-boat as the stroke-oar for 200 men. Pausing after they had rowed half a mile, they were weak, limp in body, and breathless, while his majesty was strong under his oar of twenty cubits in length. He stopped and landed his falcon-boat only after he had done three miles of rowing without interrupting his stroke. Faces shone as they saw him do this. He drew three hundred strong bows [...]. He also came to do the following which is brought to your attention: Entering his northern garden, he found erected for him four targets of Asiatic copper, of one palm in thickness, with a distance of twenty cubits between one post and the next. Then his majesty appeared on his chariot like Mont [the Egyptian god of war] in his might. He drew his bow while holding four arrows in his fist. Thus he rode northward shooting at them [...], each arrow coming out at the back of its target while he attacked the next post. It was a deed never yet done, never yet heard reported: shooting an arrow at a target of copper, so that it came out of it and dropped to the ground.

This motif is also depicted, and seems to have been handed to the Greek world where it appears in Homer's *Odyssey*, in the competition held for Penelope's suitors.

Among the different combat sports, best attested is wrestling, which was perhaps especially practiced by soldiers. Dozens of different wrestling scenes are depicted in tombs of the 12th Dynasty provincial governors of Beni Hasan in Middle Egypt, providing almost a manual of wrestling—the wrestlers are all naked, dressed only with a girdle. Other combat sports attested are stick-fencing (which is also attested in a ritual context by the Greek historian Herodotus, among others) and probably boxing. There is some evidence for actual athletic contests, such as the depiction, at Ramesses III's funerary temple at Medinet Habu, of pairs of Egyptian and foreign fighters engaged in wrestling and fencing in front of an audience of spectators. In the late Demotic tale "The Contest for the Benefice of Amun," Egyptian and (probably) Assyrian elite warriors fight with each other in front of a stand of spectators—including the pharaoh. A mythical text of the later New Kingdom that speaks about the struggle of the gods Horus and Seth for Egyptian kingship describes both a diving and a boating competition between the two gods.

We have only a little evidence about the sports that common Egyptians outside the sphere of the elite and the military practiced. One of them was probably stick-fencing, which continues to be practiced in Egypt today. There may have also been ball sports in ancient Egypt. Balls (made from wood, clay, or else from leather or linen and stuffed) are indeed attested in the archaeological record. Games involving the throwing and catching of balls are occasionally depicted, but exclusively with female players. In one of the tombs of the Middle Kingdom at Beni Hasan (mentioned above for the wrestling scenes), young men seem to play a kind of hockey, using bent-ended sticks to control a hoop, disk, or ball. In two Egyptian rituals involving balls, the king would strike a ball with a stick (to avert the evil eye of Apophis), and throw the ball into the four cardinal directions. Although board games, such as *Senet*, are known both through depictions and through examples of the actual game and pieces, we do not entirely understand how they were played as no game instructions have been found. Although certainly played for entertainment, since many games came from funerary contexts, they may also have had a religious purpose. The enduring joy of playing games across all historical and cultural time periods finds striking support in the fact that a game played by children in modern Egypt, called Labet el-Al or Bawawah, is already attested in the Egyptian New Kingdom!

8

Egyptologists

℞ 100.

Who is the most famous Egyptologist?

There are many Egyptologists well known to the broader public, as well as brilliant scholars whose fame extends only to the scholarly community, all of whom have worked on various aspects of ancient Egyptian culture over the last 200 years (see M. Bierbrier, *Who Was Who in Egyptology*). It would be a difficult task to single out just one of them. Even so, probably the most famous Egyptologist in the world today is a fictitious one (!), namely Daniel Jackson, one of the lead characters in the film *Stargate* (1994), the television series *Stargate—SG1* (1997–2007), and the film sequels *Stargate— The Ark of Truth* and *Stargate—Continuum*. The series combines parascientific and esoteric theories about Egypt with science fiction scenarios. At the beginning of the first film, Jackson is depicted as an outcast from academic Egyptology because he is convinced that ancient Egyptian culture had an extraterrestrial origin. Fictional Egyptologists—Evelyn Carnahan and Allen Chamberlain—figure prominently in two other films, *The Mummy* (1999) and *The Mummy Returns* (2001). As in the earlier version of *The Mummy* (1932), these films exploit the popular superstition that there is a "curse of the pharaohs," which is also the springboard for Philipp Vandenberg's like-named bestseller of 1975. Ancient Egypt is also the theme or background of an immense number of works of fiction, from children's books through juvenile fiction to novels for adults. Many of these novels have also lent prominence to fictional Egyptologists. In the recent bestselling trilogy of juvenile fiction, "The Kane Chronicles" by American author Rick Riordan (*The Red Pyramid, The Throne of Fire, The Serpent's Shadow,* published 2010–12), Carter and Sadie Kane—children of the famous Egyptologist and Egyptian magician Julius Kane, and descendants of Egyptian kings—find themselves face to face with Egyptian gods who have come alive again in the modern world. Another example is Arthur Phillip's novel *The Egyptologist* (2004). It features the fictitious Egyptologist Ralph M. Trilipush, marginalized in his discipline, in his desperate quest for the tomb of King Atum-Hadu and for recognition, all the while competing with (the real) Howard Carter's discovery of the tomb of Tutankhamun. Evidently, life is not easy for an Egyptologist—but perhaps you will nevertheless read the next question.

101.

Are there too many Egyptologists?

Compared with the number of university programs devoted to the study of classical antiquity (ancient Greece and Rome), those dedicated to Egyptology are quite few, indeed. Let me give you two examples, one each from Europe and North America. While the German-speaking countries have about 1,000 permanent positions dedicated to Greek and Roman culture in universities, museums, and the countries' provincial departments for the preservation of historical and archaeological heritage, there are at most 100 Egyptological positions spread among universities, museums, the academies of arts and sciences, and the German, Swiss, and Austrian Archaeological Institutes. The reasons for this discrepancy are many, and they are rooted in the importance of classical antiquity for the ideal humanistic education, the presence of Latin (and sometimes Greek) as a subject in schools, and the Roman history of Germany and the Alpine provinces. The contemporary aversion to a Eurocentric academic perspective and insight into the importance of Near Eastern cultures for the emergence of western culture has yet to trigger a diversion of resources from Classics to Near Eastern Studies, which itself comprises a whole series of individual fields. The same situation exists in North America, where around 200 programs in classical studies stand in contrast to about one-tenth that number that focus on the ancient Near East. The latter comprise not only ancient Egypt, but all the Near Eastern civilizations, and sometimes include modern cultures and languages as well.

And yet, the task confronting these few Egyptologists is a huge one. Many of the remains of the ancient culture are in danger of falling victim to modern development and to environmental change, and the requirements of some of the most important excavation sites—for instance, the huge necropolis of Saqqara and the vast area of the residence city Pi-Ramesses—exceed the available funds and personnel (see **Questions 13 and 56**). Moreover, in museum storerooms, hundreds of thousands of objects and texts have yet to be published and made accessible for scholarship. Many of these items in storage will no doubt compel us to modify our understanding of various facets of Egyptian history and culture, or even result in the rewriting of whole chapters—and this analysis will also require specialists. And, finally, there is the crucial need to disseminate this knowledge to society at large. It is especially interesting to note how different the support for scholarship can be from one country to another. In 1968, the noted French Egyptologist Serge Sauneron, who was influenced by France's centralized research policy and its focus on Paris, called for a concentration of Egyptology in five centers worldwide, rather than "diluting" the resources of the discipline among a hundred scattered, isolated, and poorly equipped institutions. Only a little earlier, in 1967, the German Egyptologist Wolfgang Helck had made precisely the opposite suggestion: since Egyptology supplies "building blocks for an understanding of the development and essence of the ancient Egyptians and their view of the world," there should be "at every university ... an Egyptologist who, with his scholarly influence, will stimulate research issues in other disciplines and supply answers to questions coming from those areas of study." It remains to be seen if (and to what degree) higher education and the wider society in the twenty-first century will provide support to Egyptology commensurate with a civilization that spanned several millennia of human history, and whose impact on the modern world is still being revealed.

Appendix

101 Reading Suggestions
for the Study of Ancient Egypt

Reception of Ancient Egypt and Modern Exploration

1. D. Wengrow, *What Makes Civilization? The Ancient Near East and the Future of the West.* Oxford: Oxford University Press, 2010.
2. E. Colla, *Conflicted Antiquities: Egyptology, Egyptomania, Egyptian Modernity.* Durham, NC: Duke University Press, 2007.
3. J.S. Curl, *The Egyptian Revival: Ancient Egypt as the Inspiration for Design Motifs in the West.* London: Routledge, 2005.
4. O. El Daly, *Egyptology: The Missing Millennium. Ancient Egypt in Medieval Arabic Writings.* London: UCL Press, 2005.
5. S. Trafton, *Egypt Land: Race and 19th Century American Egyptomania.* Durham, NC: Duke University Press, 2004.
6. S. MacDonald and M. Rice (eds), *Consuming Ancient Egypt* (Series: Encounters with Ancient Egypt). London: UCL Press, 2003.
7. J.-M. Humbert and C.A. Price, *Imhotep Today: Egyptianizing Architecture* (Series: Encounters with Ancient Egypt). London: UCL Press, 2003.
8. D. Reid, *Whose Pharaohs? Archaeology, Museums, and Egyptian National Identity from Napoleon to World War I.* Berkeley, CA: University of California Press, 2002.
9. E. Hornung, *The Secret Lore of Egypt: Its Impact on the West.* Ithaca, NY, and London: Cornell University Press, 2001.
10. J. Assmann, *Moses the Egyptian: The Memory of Egypt in Western Monotheism.* Cambridge, MA: Harvard University Press, 1997.
11. *Egyptomania: Egypt in Western Art, 1730–1930.* Ottawa: National Gallery of Canada, 1994.
12. J.S. Curl, *Egyptomania: The Egyptian Revival.* Manchester: Manchester University Press, 1994.

Ancient Egypt: General Introductions

13. A.B. Lloyd (ed.), *A Companion to Ancient Egypt*. Oxford: Wiley-Blackwell, 2010.

14. S. Ikram, *Ancient Egypt: An Introduction*. Cambridge: Cambridge University Press, 2010.

15. D.J. Brewer and E. Teeter, *Egypt and the Egyptians*. Cambridge: Cambridge University Press, 2007.

16. I. Shaw, *Ancient Egypt: A Very Short Introduction*. Oxford and New York: Oxford University Press, 2004.

17. D.B. Redford, *The Oxford Encyclopedia of Ancient Egypt (3 vols)*. Oxford and New York: Oxford University Press, 2001.

18. E. Hornung, *Idea into Image: Essays on Ancient Egyptian Thought*. New York: Timken, 1992.

19. R. Schulz and M. Seidel (eds), *Egypt: The World of the Pharaohs*. Cologne: Könemann, 1997.

20. D.P. Silverman (ed.), *Ancient Egypt*. New York: Oxford University Press, 1997.

21. I. Shaw and P. Nicholson, *The British Museum Dictionary of Ancient Egypt* (pocket ed.). London: British Museum Press, 2002. Original ed., 1995.

Egyptian History

22. Ch. Riggs (ed.), *The Oxford Handbook of Roman Egypt*. Oxford: Oxford University Press, 2012.

23. M. Van de Mieroop, *A History of Ancient Egypt*. Oxford: Wiley-Blackwell, 2011.

24. T. Wilkinson, *The Rise and Fall of Ancient Egypt*. London: Bloomsbury and New York: Random House, 2010.

25. J.G. Manning, *The Last Pharaohs: Egypt under the Ptolemies, 305–30 BC*. Princeton, NJ: Princeton University Press, 2010.

26. I. Shaw (ed.), *The Oxford History of Ancient Egypt*. Oxford: Oxford University Press, 2000.

27. R.S. Bagnall, *Egypt in the Byzantine World, 300–700*. Cambridge: Cambridge University Press, 2007.

28. B.J. Kemp, *Ancient Egypt: Anatomy of a Civilization*. 2nd ed. London: Routledge, 2006.

29. J. Assmann, *The Mind of Egypt: History and Meaning in the Time of the Pharaohs*. Cambridge, MA: Harvard University Press, 2003.

30. G. Hölbl, *A History of the Ptolemaic Empire*. London: Routledge, 2001.

31. E. Hornung, *History of Ancient Egypt: An Introduction*. Ithaca, NY, and New York: Cornell University Press, 1999.

32. T.A.H. Wilkinson, *Early Dynastic Egypt*. London: Routledge, 1999.

Egyptian Religion

33. E. Teeter, *Religion and Ritual in Ancient Egypt*. Cambridge: Cambridge University Press, 2011.

34. J. Assmann, *Death and Salvation in Ancient Egypt*. Ithaca, NY: Cornell University Press, 2005.

35. F. Dunand and C. Zivie-Coche, *Gods and Men in Egypt: 3000 BCE to 395 CE*. Ithaca, NY: Cornell University Press, 2004.

36. R.H. Wilkinson, *The Complete Gods and Goddesses of Ancient Egypt*. New York: Thames and Hudson, 2003.

37. J. Assmann, *The Search for God in Ancient Egypt*. Ithaca, NY: Cornell University Press, 2001.

38. S. Hodel-Hoenes, *Life and Death in Ancient Egypt: Scenes from Private Tombs in New Kingdom Thebes*. Ithaca, NY: Cornell University Press, 2000.

39. E. Hornung, *The Ancient Egyptian Books of the Afterlife*. Ithaca, NY, and London: Cornell University Press, 1999.

40. A. Dodson and S. Ikram, *The Mummy in Ancient Egypt*. London: Thames and Hudson, 1998.

41. S. Quirke, *The Temple in Ancient Egypt*. London: British Museum Press, 1997.

42. S. Quirke, *Ancient Egyptian Religion*. London: British Museum Press, 1992.

43. B.E. Shafer (ed.), *Religion in Ancient Egypt: Gods, Myths, and Personal Practice*. London: Routledge, 1991.

44. E. Hornung, *The Valley of the Kings: Horizon of Eternity*. Cologne: Timken, 1990.

45. E. Hornung, *Conceptions of God in Ancient Egypt: The One and The Many*. London: Routledge and Kegan Paul, 1983.

Egyptian Art, Archaeology, and Architecture

46. W. Wendrich (ed.), *Egyptian Archaeology*. Oxford: Wiley-Blackwell, 2010.

47. Z. Hawass, *Inside the Egyptian Museum with Zahi Hawass*. Cairo: The American University in Cairo Press, 2010.

48. A. Dodson and S. Ikram. *The Tomb in Ancient Egypt*. London: Thames and Hudson, 2008.

49. F. Tiradritti, *Egyptian Wall Painting*. New York: Abbeville, 2008.

50. K. Bard, *An Introduction to the Archaeology of Ancient Egypt*. Oxford: Blackwell, 2007.

51. J. Baines, *Visual and Written Culture in Ancient Egypt*. Oxford: Oxford University Press, 2007.

52. D. Arnold, *The Encyclopaedia of Ancient Egyptian Architecture*. London: I.B.Tauris, 2003.

53. M. Verner, *The Pyramids*. New York: Grove Press, 2001.
54. J. Málek, *Egyptian Art*. London: Phaidon Press, 2000.
55. N. Reeves, *Ancient Egypt: The Great Discoveries. A Year-by-Year Chronicle*. London: Thames and Hudson, 2000.
56. A. Dodson, *After the Pyramids: The Valley of the Kings and Beyond*. Ontario: Rubicon, 2000.
57. F. Tiradritti, *The Cairo Museum—Masterpieces of Egyptian Art*. London: Thames and Hudson, 1999.
58. D. Arnold, *Temples of the Last Pharaohs*. New York: Oxford University Press, 1999.
59. W.S. Smith, *The Art and Architecture of Ancient Egypt* (rev. ed. by W.K. Simpson). New Haven, CT, and London: Yale University Press, 1998.
60. G. Robins, *The Art of Ancient Egypt*. London: British Museum Press, 1997.
61. M. Lehner, *The Complete Pyramids*. London: Thames and Hudson, 1997.
62. N. Reeves, *The Complete Valley of the Kings*. London: Thames and Hudson, 1996.
63. I.E.S. Edwards, *The Pyramids of Egypt*. London: Penguin, 1993.
64. R.H. Wilkinson, *Reading Egyptian Art*. New York: Thames and Hudson, 1992.

Egyptian Language and Literature

65. J.P. Allen, *Middle Egyptian: An Introduction to the Language and Culture of Hieroglyphs*. 2nd ed. Cambridge: Cambridge University Press, 2010.
66. B. Ockinga, *A Concise Grammar of Middle Egyptian*. 2nd rev. ed. Mainz: Philip von Zabern, 2005.
67. P. Wilson, *Hieroglyphs: A Very Short Introduction*. Oxford: Oxford University Press, 2004.
68. M. Collier and B. Manley, *How to Read Egyptian Hieroglyphs*. 2nd ed. London: British Museum Press, 2004.
69. J. Hoch, *Middle Egyptian Grammar*. Mississauga: Benben Publications, 1997.
70. A. Loprieno, *Ancient Egyptian: A Linguistic Introduction*. Cambridge: Cambridge University Press, 1995.
71. R.B. Parkinson, *Poetry and Culture in Middle Kingdom Egypt: A Dark Side to Perfection*. London: Equinox, 2010.
72. R.B. Parkinson, *Reading Ancient Egyptian Poetry: Among Other Histories*. Malden, MA: Wiley-Blackwell, 2009.
73. M. Lichtheim, *Ancient Egyptian Literature: A Book of Readings*. 3 vols. Berkeley, CA: University of California Press, 1973–1980. Reprinted 2006.

74. W.K. Simpson (ed.), *The Literature of Ancient Egypt: An Anthology of Stories, Instructions, Stelae, Autobiographies, and Poetry.* 3rd ed. New Haven, CT: Yale University Press, 2003.
75. K.A. Kitchen, *Poetry of Ancient Egypt.* Gothenburg: Åström, 1999.
76. R.B. Parkinson, *The Tale of Sinuhe and Other Ancient Egyptian Poems.* Oxford: Oxford University Press, 1998.
77. A. Loprieno (ed.), *Ancient Egyptian Literature: History and Forms.* Leiden: Brill, 1996.

Egyptian Society

78. W. Grajetzki, *The Middle Kingdom of Ancient Egypt: History, Archaeology, and Society.* London: Duckworth, 2006.
79. A.J. Spalinger, *War in Ancient Egypt: The New Kingdom.* Oxford: Blackwell, 2005.
80. B.J. Kemp, *Ancient Egypt: Anatomy of a Civilization.* Rev. ed., London: Routledge, 2005.
81. A. Dodson and D. Hilton, *The Complete Royal Families of Ancient Egypt.* London: Thames and Hudson, 2004.
82. D.B. Redford, *From Slave to Pharaoh: The Black Experience of Ancient Egypt.* Baltimore, MD: Johns Hopkins University Press, 2004.
83. L. Meskell, *Private Life in New Kingdom Egypt.* Princeton, NJ, and Oxford: Princeton University Press, 2002.
84. A.G. McDowell, *Village Life in Ancient Egypt: Laundry Lists and Love Songs.* Oxford: Oxford University Press, 2001.
85. L. Meskell, *Archaeologies of Social Life: Age, Sex, Class et cetera in Ancient Egypt.* Oxford and Malden, MA: Blackwell, 1999.
86. S. Donadoni (ed.) *The Egyptians.* Chicago, IL, and London: Chicago University Press, 1997.
87. G. Robins, *Women in Ancient Egypt.* London: British Museum Press, 1993.
88. E. Strouhal, *Life in Ancient Egypt.* Cambridge: Cambridge University Press, 1992.
89. W. Decker, *Sport and Games in Ancient Egypt.* New Haven, CT, and London: Yale University Press, 1992.
90. L. Manniche, *Music and Musicians in Ancient Egypt.* London: British Museum Press, 1991.
91. L. Manniche, *Sexual Life in Ancient Egypt.* London and New York: Routledge and Kegan Paul, 1987.

Amarna Period

92. A. Dodson, *Amarna Sunset: Nefertiti, Tutankhamun, Ay, Horemheb, and the Egyptian Counter-reformation*. Cairo: The American University in Cairo Press, 2009.
93. Z. Hawass, *King Tutankhamun: The Treasures of the Tomb*. London: Thames and Hudson, 2008.
94. D.P. Silverman, J.W. Wegner, and J. Houser Wegner, *Akhenaten and Tutankhamun: Revolution and Restoration*. Philadelphia, PA: University of Pennsylvania, Museum of Archaeology and Anthropology, 2006.
95. C.N. Reeves, *Akhenaten: Egypt's False Prophet*. London: Thames and Hudson, 2001.
96. D. Montserrat, *Akhenaten: History, Fantasy, and Ancient Egypt*. London: Routledge, 2000.
97. R.E. Freed (ed.), *Pharaohs of the Sun: Akhenaten, Nefertiti, Tutankhamen*. Catalogue Museum of Fine Arts, Boston. London: Thames and Hudson, 1999.
98. E. Hornung, *Akhenaten and the Religion of Light*. Ithaca, NY: Cornell University Press, 1999.
99. N. Reeves, *The Complete Tutankhamun: The King, The Tomb, The Royal Treasure*. London: Thames and Hudson, 1990.

Egyptologists

100. M. Bierbrier, *Who Was Who in Egyptology*. London: Egypt Exploration Society, 2012.
101. R.H. Wilkinson (ed.), *Egyptology Today*. Cambridge: Cambridge University Press, 2008.